The Real Estate Investing Copywriter's Playbook

Do More Real Estate Deals With These Proven Step-By-Step Marketing Strategies

Aaron Hoos
RealEstateInvestingCopywriter.com

THE REAL ESTATE INVESTING COPYWRITER'S PLAYBOOK

Copyright © 2018 Aaron Hoos

THIS BOOK IS OWNED EXCLUSIVELY BY THE COPYRIGHT HOLDER. NO PART OF THIS BOOK MAY BE COPIED, DISTRIBUTED, OR SOLD WITHOUT WRITTEN AUTHORIZATION FROM THE COPYRIGHT HOLDER.

THE CONTENT OF THIS BOOK IS FOR INFORMATIONAL PURPOSES ONLY AND PRESENTED TO A WIDE AUDIENCE WITH THE EXPECTATION THAT ALL READERS WILL FIRST CONSULT WITH LICENSED PROFESSIONALS WHO CAN PROVIDE SPECIFIC GUIDANCE.

ALL FINANCIAL DETAILS, NUMBERS, PRICES, AND CASE STUDIES ARE PROVIDED AS EXAMPLES ONLY. PAST PERFORMANCE DOES NOT GUARANTEE FUTURE RESULTS.

NO GUARANTEE OR WARRANTY OF ANY KIND IS OFFERED OR IMPLIED. READERS ACCEPT ALL LIABILITY FOR THEIR ACTIONS.

All rights reserved.

ISBN-13: 978-1523969180
ISBN-10: 1523969180

DEDICATION

For Janelle

CONTENTS

Foreword By Trevor Mauch	9
Foreword By Mark Evans DM,DN	11
Introduction	13
Chapter 1: My Manifesto On Marketing, Copywriting, And Selling, And Why These Skills Are Absolutely Essential For Every Real Estate Investor	19
PART 1: YOUR MARKET	**23**
Chapter 2: Your Target Audience (The Starting Point For The Most Profitable Marketing)	24
Chapter 3: WIIFM+ROI=$$$	35
Chapter 4: Competition	40
PART 2: YOUR BRAND	**49**
Chapter 5: Specialization And Differentiation	50
Chapter 6: Your Story, Character, And Voice	59
Chapter 7: Your Brand	68

CONTENTS

PART 3: YOUR BUSINESS — 75

Chapter 8: Your Business Model — 76

Chapter 9: Your Sales Funnel — 80

Chapter 10: Your Marketing — 93

PART 4: CREATE AND DEPLOY YOUR MARKETING — 97

Chapter 11: Different Types Of Marketing And How To Use Them — 98

Chapter 12: The Science Of Copywriting — 105

Chapter 13: The Copywriting Power Matrix — 116

Chapter 14: Action Plan: How To Build And Deploy Everything In This Book To Get It Working For You — 143

Chapter 15: The 4 Step Sequence To Implement Everything Confidently And Grow Your Investing Business — 147

CONTENTS

PART 5: BEST PRACTICES   155

Chapter 16: Best Practices And Effective Strategies For Marketing To Sellers   156

Chapter 17: Best Practices And Effective Strategies For Marketing To Buyers   162

Now It's Time To Take Action…   167

About Aaron Hoos   170

Connect With The Real Estate Investing Copywriter   171

FOREWORD BY TREVOR MAUCH

Years ago when I got my start as an entrepreneur I went down the same path most of us do.

I'd look at what others were doing in my market, create my version of it, and let 'er fly hoping it would make the impact I'd want to make.

But I quickly found out that there was way more to marketing and cracking through that clutter with your business than tossing up a pretty page, creating a visually striking mail piece, or just modeling the "structure" of someone else's marketing hoping it would work for me too.

The part I was ignoring at first was actually the most important piece of the marketing. The part that 8 out of 10 real estate entrepreneurs ignore at the detriment of their business.

It's the actual words on the page.

A mentor once told me a great analogy that really cemented the power of words.

Imagine you have a $1 bill in one hand... and a $100 bill in the other.

They're both printed on pretty much the same paper. With the same ink, maybe even on the same printing press. They look pretty similar in design, color, structure... from 10 feet away you really can't easily distinguish many differences in the two.

But one of those pieces of paper is worth 100x more than the other one.

What's the primary difference that makes it worth more? It's simply the words on the paper.

The words in your marketing can be the difference between you cutting through that clutter or being a part of the clutter. They can be the difference between your business making it vs. struggling. They can be the difference between your marketing campaign turning a massive profit or doing in the red.

Once I learned the importance of learning the skillset of turning words into sales (copywriting) that's when my businesses started to grow. In some cases here at Carrot we've changed 5 words on a page that instantly connected with our clients better that increased our results by over 50%.

Aaron has worked with Carrot and dozens of our top clients over the years and he's the go-to specialist for real estate investing copy. He's a master when it comes to crafting high performing copy.

THE REAL ESTATE INVESTING COPYWRITER'S PLAYBOOK

Dive into every page of this book and take notes, be a student of copywriting, and find ways to apply it not only to your real estate business but to every part of your life.

I promise you when you learn this skillset it can be one of the most valuable skillsets you have in your business.

Trevor Mauch
Founder and CEO of InvestorCarrot

My note back to Trevor:

Thank you, Trevor! You are a great example to me of someone who builds an amazing business that is focused on helping people at the highest levels. In fact, as I think about growing my copywriting business and my investing business, I often think of conversation we've had on the phone, and I replay those word-for-word in my mind and gain insight from them. You have a great team and a great service, and I recommend InvestorCarrot to *everyone*.

-Aaron

Want to learn more about Trevor and InvestorCarrot? Just reach out to me at aaron@realestateinvestingcopywriter.com and ask! I would be happy to connect you with the InvestorCarrot team.

And if you want to know how my clients use InvestorCarrot, or if you want additional copywriting or blog posts for your InvestorCarrot website, get in touch and let me know that you're an InvestorCarrot member!

FOREWORD BY MARK EVANS DM,DN

Have you ever wanted to run a business from the beach? That was a goal of mine and achieved it. Aaron was part of that journey. Here's how I did it...

I was born and raised in Ohio, and ran my businesses there. Although my family is there and I was raised there, I've always preferred a different climate and approach to life: I wanted to live on the beach; I wanted to travel the world.

But when you run a business, it's only natural to feel "stuck" to the location where your business is, and during those dark and snowy Columbus winters I wondered what I could do to escape (without wrecking my business in the process).

Then one day I realized that it wasn't a matter of choosing one or the other; I could have both: I could build a business that operated in Ohio (or whatever other markets I chose) while I operated it virtually from a distance.

And so, in 2005, I packed up my belongings and moved to warm and sunny South Beach, Florida with my then-fiance (now my wife) Deena.

It was a test to see if I could live in a different place than my business and run it from there. If it worked, I could go on to the second phase of my dream, to travel the world while my business continued to run.

I started putting the pieces in place to run a business from a distance. One of the challenges I needed to solve was communicate to my buyers' list and marketing to grow that list.

You see, while many investors focus on finding sellers (and then struggle to find cash buyers), I approached it differently. In my "virtual" real estate business I wanted to build a massive list of cash buyers who wanted to create good returns with real estate without all the headaches so they would invest in cash-flowing properties that I had in my portfolio. I knew that content marketing, copywriting, and book writing/publishing would be vital components of building my brand and business from a distance.

And that's when I met Aaron. I found him online and got him to work on a small project for me.

What started out as a small editing job on one project turned into another project, then another, then another. Before long, he was taking care of a number of writing and marketing projects for me—handling not only the writing or editing, but also the underlying content strategy and sometimes the implementation too.

And while he wrote, my business grew. I travelled the world with Deena for 7 years, staying connected with my business and with Aaron by email and phone. I held events all over the US. I married Deena, and she and I had a son, Mark III. Aaron stayed on my Contact List the whole time as one of my go-to vendors to help me as I ran my business and lived my life.

As I write this, we've worked together for 13 years and counting. He's not only been my writer but he's become my friend and client too. Over the years he's written or edited a lot of my work, from blogs to social posts, from books to info-products, from emails to direct mail, and more. We've gone on to collaborate on a couple of projects, he's invested in real estate from me and attended my events, and I've referred a number of clients to him.

If you run a real estate investing business, and if you know the power of content marketing and copywriting to build your business, then this book can give you the foundation you need to get to the next level.

Just don't hire Aaron to do your writing because I need him to work on something for me! ;)

Mark Evans DM,DN
MarkEvansDM.com

My note back to Mark:

Wow, dude! Thank you. I've done a lot of real estate investing stuff in the past but when I think about my start as a real estate investing *copywriter*, you are key to that transformation in my life. I love working with you, and we do some amazing things together. Hey, let's write something else together soon… text me when you're ready to hop on the phone!

-Aaron

Want to learn more about Mark and his business? Whether you're a cash buyer or an investor who wants to go virtual, Mark can help. Just reach out to me at aaron@realestateinvestingcopywriter.com and if I think there's a fit, I will happily make an introduction to his business.

INTRODUCTION

Waaaay back when I was just 13 years old, I wanted a "real" job. One that paid me a regular paycheck. So I jumped onto my BMX bike and pedaled down the rural road that my family lived on, to the nearest place that I knew was hiring: a race track. It wasn't a local racetrack; it was a big track that had been on the Formula 1 circuit (and, in fact, even today the NASCAR Truck series still races there sometimes).

I got a job on the grounds crew, keeping the place clean and running errands for staffers. I was paid maybe $3.00 or $4.00 an hour and, of course, got to see races for free!

And that started my life-long interest in autosports.

The reason why I'm telling you this is because of what I learned about autosports over the years inspires how I think about real estate investing: You don't have to love racing as much as I do to appreciate the lesson here…

In racing, a driver and a car both work together. Both need to be finely-tuned high-performance machines that operate in sync. If either one is not working properly, they will not win the race.

And here's how that ties into real estate investing: many investors get into investing because they like real estate and they want to achieve financial freedom so they can quit their 9-5 jobs and spend more time with family. Yet, what many investors don't realize is that they are building a *business*.

Investors often focus on the houses and on the passive cash flow, but they don't focus on the business as a whole. To use an autosports analogy, if the investor is like a racecar driver and their investing business is like a racecar, how well do you think the investor will perform if they work hard themselves but don't focus on building their business? That's like a racecar driver staying in great shape but ignoring how well their car will drive… or, worse yet, thinking that they can win a race by not even driving a car.

I see many hard-working real estate investors do just that—and, predictably, they struggle, burn out, and even fail because they get focused on finding houses with cash flow potential yet ignore the *business* side of it. They work hard to find a few properties and don't realize that building a business allows them scale that business to do more deals—if only they start thinking of their investing business as a business. But my clients, who are among some of the leading investors in the country, work at a high level and focus on their *business*—just like a racecar driver who makes sure that their racecar can perform at the level they need it to perform at.

My work as a real estate investing copywriter is to help high performance investors build the high performance investing machine they need. My work is to help them build that business that allows them to scale up so they're not running around trying to put one deal together but rather building a business (while maintaining their sanity) to do multiple deals without stress.

I don't "just" write copy for my investing clients. I'm not an vending machine that churns out whatever copy I'm asked to write. Rather, I use copy, as well as content strategy and content marketing, across a wide variety of channels, to help investors focus and grow their business.

My work is to shift my clients' thinking from "*I'm an investor who buys and sells houses*" to "*I'm a high-performance investor building a high-performance business*" (of which copywriting and marketing is an essential part).

There are a few key differentiators between those two mindsets I just described—differentiators like systems and structures and delegation—but the biggest differentiators that I deal with are strategies like branding, marketing, lead-generation, sales funnels, and more.

For those who can book a phone appointment with me (not always easy to do; I'm a busy guy), you'll quickly find out that I'm not really about taking a "one-off" job for a couple thousand bucks because you need an email sequence. My approach is much more about figuring out what is happening in your business now, what your goals are, and how my copywriting (and marketing strategy) can help you achieve those goals. I'm the guy who will help you turn your "*I just invest in houses*" into a high-performance investment *business*.

That's why I wrote this book: because there are many investors who might be wondering how to find more sellers or buyers, or they might be wondering how to go from one or two deals to multiple deals, or they might be wondering how to automate and delegate so they're not the only ones doing everything, or they might be wondering grow their business, or they might be wondering if they need to bring a marketing person on board. I want to empower investors to figure out what they want to achieve and how copywriting and marketing might help them achieve it.

Over the last two decades (has it really been that long?!? Yikes!) I have pulled together TONS of material about copywriting, sales, marketing, psychology, and consumer behavior into gigantic shelf (and filing cabinet and Dropbox folder) of reference material.

It's highly effective and laser-targeted on real estate investors.

And now, I'm giving away a lot of that secret sauce in the next several chapters! Why am I doing it? Well, for a couple of reasons…

First, because I've learned that not everyone can afford my services but they still need good copy. And I believe that by equipping those people to grow big, successful investing businesses, maybe they'll be able to invest in my services in the future to write even higher-level stuff.

Second, because even those who can hire me often want to know my process, just to understand how I work. Some will read this book before they work with me to see what my approach will be like; others my read this book after they work with me to see how else they want to grow.

I'm more than happy to share some of that here—yes, even the proprietary stuff—because it makes us all more successful (and don't worry, I still have a few tricks up my sleeve that I haven't shared here).

My Story (And The Lessons It Can Teach Investors)

I didn't start out as a real estate investor or a copywriter. I kind of fell into both.

From an early age I was exposed to the real estate investing industry. My dad was a contractor who sometimes worked for investors and would bring me along to his job sites. (I didn't like it at the time although now I regret not paying more attention—sorry dad!) I did help a bit, and later, I would help a relative build an investment property from the ground up. During college I worked for a developer as he built a brand new subdivision. After college I landed a job for a real estate investing firm working in their administrative department. Without realizing it and without any plan or intention, I glimpsed inside the real estate investing industry from many angles; I saw the good, bad, and ugly. I learned what worked and what didn't, purely by accident.

Through it all, I never wanted to be a real estate investor. My exposure had always been as the sweaty, dust-covered guy with a hammer or the laser level. Not fun; it was purely done because of family relationships or for the money. Instead, I dreamed of being a writer. That's where my real skill was. So I started down the road toward becoming a newspaper journalist (which was kind of a default job that seemed like it would be a fit for someone who wanted to write but didn't want to write novels). Fortunately, I discovered early that I hated journalism—I felt like an ambulance chaser as I looked for the bad news (because that's the only news printed).

Slowly, though, these two paths of real estate investing and writing intersected. I started writing marketing content and sales copy. And, at the same time, the industries I worked in grew narrower and narrow: at first I wrote for anyone, and then I wrote for financial and real estate professionals, and then finally I narrowed my focus even further when I realized that I absolutely loved working with real estate investors.

Today, I'm a real estate investing copywriter and a real estate investor. (Hey, you gotta walk the talk, right?) I write copy (mostly direct response copy but occasionally I'll write other things if you can convince me) for real estate investors. I have a team of specialist writers who write other content that my clients need, such as social media or other content marketing.

Here's why that matters: For 30 years or more I've been involved in different ways with the real estate investing industry. For nearly 20 years I've been writing for real estate investors. For the last 10+ I've written sales copy almost exclusively for real estate investors. I've met a lot of investors around the world. I've worked with a lot of them, too—from the ones you never hear about to the ones that everyone knows (and you've probably read their books and bought their courses and attended their events).

Along the way I've learned a lot. Not just about copywriting but about running a real estate investing *business*. Now, I'm not here to tell you about how to set up and run your business—I'll leave that to the gurus. But I do have one advantage to offer you that the gurus don't: I have seen literally thousands of real estate investing businesses—some that worked and some that didn't—and I've paid attention and made copious notes.

And, I've learned something that is common among all real estate investors, whether they are brand new or one of the big-name industry leaders: Their copy is part of the story of their success; what's even more important is the sales funnel. (Yeah, I hate to admit that there's something more important than the copy but it's true. A real estate investor's sales funnel is far, far more important than even the copy I write for them).

If you have great copy but a horrible sales funnel, your business is doomed. But if you have a great sales funnel, you can get away with mediocre copy (your business won't be perfect but at least you have a starting point).

(Interestingly, this is actually a third path of my life that has intersected with investing and copywriting because when studying for an MBA, I wrote my thesis on sales funnels, which later became my first book, *The Sales Funnel Bible*).

So, real estate investing, copywriting, and sales funnels have culminated into this book that you're now reading.

I am privileged to work on copywriting and sales funnels for investors. It's not something I have to do; it's something I love to do.

Let's Start Working On Your Real Estate Investing

The "work" of a real estate investor is not easy. If it were easy, everyone would do it. Although real estate investing can be done anywhere (and is preferable to fighting commuter traffic to go to a JOB), real estate investing is still not necessarily easy. There are strategies and tactics to consider, new ventures to pursue, catastrophic problems to mitigate.

In this book, I want to show you how to stack the odds in your favor; how to lean toward success by building a real estate investing business that runs like a high performance machine.

In this book, I'm going to talk about what a real estate investing sales funnel is and why it's important. (So, if you've been reading about this "sales funnel" but aren't sure what it is, don't worry… I'll cover it). And I'll talk about what you need to do to build a great sales funnel in your investing business (actually, you'll have more than one; I'll talk about that, too). I'll show you some sales funnels that work and give you some variations on each one so you can make it your own. And, I'll give you some advanced strategies to take your sales funnel – and ultimately your business – to the next level.

Then we'll talk about copywriting and marketing. I'll help you build a strategy that makes sense for your situation (no matter what kind of investing you do), and I'll get really tactical with a step-by-step plan of how to implement your customized strategy to grow your investing business.

Whether you have an existing and successful real estate investing business right now, or if you are just starting out and still trying to figure out what you want to do… and, whether you are a wholesaler or rehabber or cash flow investor or note investor or an expert looking for an audience (or any other type of investor), you'll find my best strategies in this book.

Here's what I recommend: make sure you take action on each chapter. You'll learn the solid basics of branding, sales funnels, content marketing, and more, so you can grow from whatever point you're at right now.

Let's roll up our sleeves and work on building your real estate investing business into a fine-tuned high performance business that will grow and serve your life.

BONUS: I've created a ton of bonuses and downloadable resources that accompany this book. They include templates, examples, links to other resources or even recommendations of people I love to work with. You don't *need* them to read through the book but they'll often add value. RealEstateInvestingCopywriter.com/bonus/playbookbonus

THE REAL ESTATE INVESTING COPYWRITER'S PLAYBOOK

Just a couple more quick notes about the book...

Terminology

You'll notice that I often use the words "sellers" and "buyers". However, I recognize that there are many different ways to invest in real estate and you may have a different type of seller or buyer than the example I give. The information still applies, so adjust as necessary.

Also, sometimes I use the word "client" or "marketplace" in this book. The sellers and buyers you work with are your clients (even though investors rarely think in those terms); and, the zip codes you work in is your marketplace. I use these terms generically due to the wide variety of investors I work with. Again, adjust as necessary.

Some Assembly Required

I wrote this to help investors of all types and levels of experience. But there's only one way this book will actually help you: if you do the work in the book. I've given you the strategies, and put them in a logical sequence. So just start at the beginning and go through chapter-by-chapter and follow the steps. That's it. I can't reiterate this enough.

Services Available

I offer copywriting services but there's nothing in this book that requires you to hire me. In fact, I purposely wrote this book because many investors can't hire me... or because they've hired someone else and now need to figure out what's working and what isn't.

I don't take on very many clients anymore (because I'm often fully booked) but the best way to see if we are a fit to work together, and to see if I have availability to accept any additional projects, is to join my VIP list at RealEstateInvestingCopywriter.com/join.

And, if you already have copy that you're using (or if you can't afford to work with me so you hired a copywriter who fit within your budget) and you just want a second opinion on some existing copy, you can book one of my copy critiques at RealEstateInvestingCopywriter.com/copycritique.

Either way, I hope we get to work together!

CHAPTER 1: MY MANIFESTO ON MARKETING, COPYWRITING, AND SELLING, AND WHY THESE SKILLS ARE ABSOLUTELY ESSENTIAL FOR EVERY REAL ESTATE INVESTOR

Investors get into investing because they love real estate. Or they love helping people. Or they love making money. Or they love the idea of passive cash flow. Or all of the above.

They'll think about how to do deals (Wholesaling? Flipping? Buy-and-holds? There are many different ways) and from there they'll start investing.

It's only later that they realize there are other pieces they need to think about: teams... systems... financials... technology... *marketing*...

Marketing (plus the more focused functions of marketing, like copywriting, social media promotion, branding, etc.) is often an afterthought to investors. But it doesn't take long for investors to soon discover just how essential this marketing/copywriting/selling skill is to their business.

- Copywriting is important when you send out a postcard to find a motivated seller.
- Copywriting is important when a motivated seller calls you back in response to your postcard.
- Copywriting is important when you're face-to-face with a seller to convince them to sell their house to you.
- Copywriting is important when you're looking for tenants.
- Copywriting is important when you build a list of cash buyers who can buy this property and many others that you hope to sell or wholesale.
- Copywriting is important when you build relationships with referral partners.
- Copywriting is important when you are building a brand so you can scale up your business from being focused on individual transactions to turn your business into a team-effort that does multiple deals.
- Copywriting is important when you build even further to grow a brand that teaches other investors who to invest.

- Copywriting important when you are trying to improve all of the above aspects of your business so you can do more deals, faster, and more profitably, branch into more lines of business, and do it all with less stress (and perhaps even from the comfort of your bathrobe).

It's ALL marketing; it's ALL copywriting; it's ALL selling. So, when a prospective client gets on the phone with me and asks "what kind of copy do you write?" I often say: "anything that you need in your investing business—from direct mail to sales letters, from social media to video scripts, from blog posts to email, from ebooks to books—it's ALL marketing/copywriting/selling. All of it works together to lead the motivated seller or cash buyer (or whoever you're doing business with) on a journey toward doing a deal with you.

There are some copywriters out there who focus just on direct response (such as postcards and emails) and that is a very specific skillset. I have that skillset but I also know something they don't: blog posts and social media posts aren't some frivolous throwaway content that doesn't matter. It should all work together.

Let me show you why I believe that:

Think about what all of your marketing/copywriting/selling efforts must do: At the most basic level, your marketing must capture the attention of the prospect (whether that prospect is a motivated seller, cash buyer, or anything else), your marketing must explain why they should do business with you versus anyone else, and your marketing must get them to take action right away. When all three of those things happen, you'll do deals.

Not all of your marketing and copy does all of those things in the same amount every single time. However, all of your marketing and copy needs work together, with *each of them* doing *some* of those things *some* of the time… and it all works together. Just like how various pieces of a car won't work on their own but when you put them together you can get where you want to go.

I believe marketing, copywriting, and selling has three functions:

- **Connect** with your audience to capture their attention
- **Convince** your audience why they should do business with you
- **Convert** your audience by getting them to take action

And you can see how they work together in the following diagram…

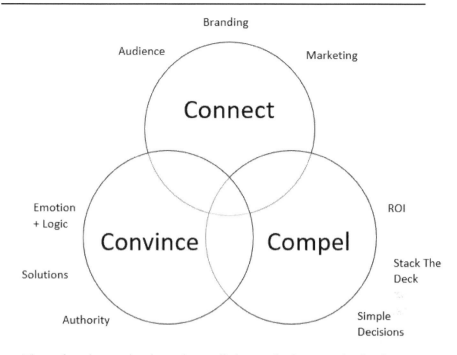

These functions exist throughout all the marketing you do. In the very early stages of getting the attention of a motivated seller or cash buyer, you're doing more **connecting**. As you build a relationship with them, you're **convincing** them by establishing your authority and credibility as the best person possible to help them. As you draw closer to a deal, you're **converting** them. But even when you are converting someone, you're still continuing to connect with them and convince them.

Therefore, all of your marketing, copy, and sales efforts need to work together to achieve those three things.

So, let's use a common example that many investors will understand:

1. You send out some postcards to a list, hoping to find some motivated sellers who will sell you their house for a below-market price. Your postcards need to do a lot of **connecting**, as well as some **convincing**, and some **converting** (although at this point you only need to convert them on why they should call you back).
2. Once on the phone with the people who have called you back, you still need to keep **connecting** with them a bit to establish rapport, but you need to do more **convincing** that you're the right person to help them, and then you need to start **converting** them on why you should come to their house to give them an offer.
3. And maybe some of them want to learn more about you so they visit your website to check out your blogs and to watch some

YouTube videos that you recorded, both of which need to **connect**, **convince**, and **convert** as well!
4. At their house, you meet with them and hand them some educational material and forms. Your printed material plus your in-person sales skills will continue to do some **connecting** (to continue establishing rapport) and some **convincing** (to continue showing them why you are the best person to help them) but a lot of **converting** to turn them into a deal.

This is just one example of working with a motivated seller but these connect, convince, convert functions need to happen in ALL of your marketing, copywriting, and selling efforts, and they need to happen with each of the groups of people you work with (including motivated sellers, cash buyers, tenants, students, and anyone else).

Therefore, when someone asks me what kind of copy I write, the answer is: I (and my team) write it all because it all needs to work together to connect with your audiences, convince them to work with you, and then convert them into deals.

You will see how these concepts play out in every single chapter in this book, from your branding to your sales funnel, from the copywriting to the social media, every single piece of every single chapter needs to do these three things.

If you're a real estate investor who wants to grow, and you're not sure where to start, just take a look at everything you do and say your various seller and buyer audiences, and figure out how you can connect, convince, and convert them more effectively. Make *that* work your daily work as an investor—and do it for both sellers and buyers and anyone else you need to work with—and you will grow your business.

BONUS: I've created a bonus resource to help you use the Connect/Convince/Compel diagram (from earlier in this chapter) to create more effective marketing in your investing business! Get it at: RealEstateInvestingCopywriter.com/bonus/playbookbonus

PART 1: YOUR MARKET

I'm sure you're eager to jump right into marketing so you can start generating leads and then turn those leads into deals. While many investors do that, it's actually a costly mistake because it skips over critical information that you need in order to market effectively.

Many investors just blanket an area with postcards and then get frustrated by the lack of responses. But savvy investors know better. They know that the "market" in "marketing" is the key. It all starts with understanding your market and figuring out what they want to hear.

By the end of Part 1 you'll have a deep understanding of the clients you will be working with and the tools and ways of thinking that will help you create marketing that converts. (Hint: the more time you spend in Part 1, the better equipped you'll be as you continue through the other Parts of this book.)

CHAPTER 2: YOUR TARGET AUDIENCE (THE STARTING POINT FOR THE MOST PROFITABLE MARKETING)

The starting point of any piece of marketing is NOT what you want to get out of your marketing efforts; it's NOT how you plan to deliver that marketing to your audience; it's NOT the kind of investing that you do.

Rather, the starting point of any piece of marketing is: your intended audience; the people who you want to see and respond to your marketing.

Who will receive this marketing? What are they thinking when they open their mailbox or their email inbox? What motivates them to take action? What kinds of actions are they likely to take? What objections might they have?

Before you decide on any kind of marketing, consider first who your audience will be and make sure you have clearly defined who should be seeing and responding to your marketing.

Unfortunately, this very first point is often overlooked, ignored, or glossed over by investors because they believe that they need to reach as many people as possible.

The misguided thinking goes: "rather than invest a significant amount of money on a small audience of people to really connect with them, I should spend the same amount to speak more broad to a larger audience because I might be able to connect with even more people."

I see it all the time when I work with investors. The investor sees the number of people they *should be* connecting with on a small, focused list, and then they see the number of people they *could be* connecting with on a larger, unfocused list; many investors say: maybe we should generalize the message a bit to reach more people.

It's a very common way to think but the math doesn't hold up. It almost always makes more sense to narrow your audience and work with a small group of people. Here's why…

Think of an advertisement for a car. Imagine what kind of ad it would be if it tried to reach everyone: The ad would need to show how the car was perfect for the snowy conditions of Norway or the desert conditions of the Sahara; the ad would need to show how the car was affordable for the young college student yet luxurious for the wealthy business owner; the ad would need to show how the car was safe for the growing family with young children yet sporty for the people who liked to race; the car would need to be available in every color because everyone wants to choose their own color; it would need to show both the right-hand drive and left-hand drive for the countries where each are required...

Oh, and the ad would need to be in every language in the world.

I hope you're laughing at how silly that kind of ad would be. It's impractical. And no one would buy that car based on that ad because you can't be all things to all people in marketing. Even by publishing an ad in English, you are eliminating billions of potential customers.

To create effective marketing you need to limit your audience to a laser-focused target audience and speak only to them.

This is easy for me to say and it's easy for most investors to agree with in principle but when it comes time to spend your marketing dollars on postcards and website design, many investors fold under the pressure and try to reach as broad an audience as possible. But that's a mistake.

You'll *think* you're spending more money to reach fewer people but what you're really doing by narrowing your audience in a laser-focused way is spending slightly more now for quantifiably larger results.

That's the conundrum that every investor faces: you can spend less on wide-reaching broad-audience marketing but it won't be as effective; or you can spend slightly more up-front to create vastly more effective marketing.

Don't make the mistake of thinking that you're getting "more affordable" marketing by reaching a wider audience! More affordable marketing is marketing that works to bring in deals, and THAT kind of marketing costs more *up-front* to reach a narrower audience but it's ultimately the most affordable marketing because it creates the larger return on investment in the long-run.

The better path to doing more deals for less work and lower cost (and more profit!) is to understand your audience at a deeper level, to "get inside their head" and know exactly what they're thinking and feeling (even before they're thinking and feeling it!). When you do this, powerful things happen: you create better sales and marketing copy, you'll communicate with them more effectively on the phone and in person, you'll build better marketing programs, you'll write more helpful blog posts, and you may even find (as some of my clients have found) that you could end up totally changing what your offer is and how you sell it... based entirely on who your audience REALLY is (even if you never noticed before).

As an example, if you are a wholesaler looking for motivated sellers, it can be tempting to send out a mass mailed postcard and hope to find burnt out landlords, elderly people with lots of equity who want to downsize, and people in financial distress. However, there aren't many postcards that speak to all three audiences with equal effectiveness. You'll end up getting fewer calls back because none of your three target audiences really feel that the postcard is speaking to them or offering to solve their unique problem.

So, I want to share a strategy I use whenever someone hires me to write copy for them. I've developed a step-by-step system to research, analyze, and create a very insight Audience Profile—a profile that helps you know your audience at the deepest levels. I use this to write copy that resonates with the reader and compels them to act.

Smart, effective, and profitable marketing begins by identifying your target audience and building ALL marketing to speak to that group alone.

Use this profiling method for each audience you have. For example, if you're an investor who works with motivated sellers, cash buyers, private lenders, and investing students, then you've got 4 different audiences to start with. And there's a good chance, as you dig into this, that you may have even more: for example, you might have an audience of motivated sellers who have inherited property and a different audience of motivated sellers who are going through foreclosure—those may be two different motivated seller audiences.

The Real Estate Investing Copywriter Audience Profiling System

Connecting with your target market (both sellers AND buyers) is the fastest way to do more deals, get more money, and grow your business. Here is how to identity, understand, and connect with your target market in 5 steps. So, choose a target market (i.e. sellers, buyers, students, and preferably even more specific than that) and follow along in these steps. Then do this for as many audiences as you have...

Step 1.—Demographics: The first step is to list the demographics of your target market. These are the very basic characteristics that are common among the majority of your target market. Yes, there will always be exceptions but focus on the general majority of your audience. I like the following list, although there might be some questions that don't apply or that you simply cannot find the answers to.

- Location where they live
- Location where they own/invest (if different)
- Age
- Gender
- Ethnicity
- Religion
- Income

- Employment
- Education
- Marital status
- Children
- Hobbies/Past-times
- Level of experience with this transaction

These are the basic demographic characteristics that make up your target market. The more details you have, the better, but I realize that not all of this information will be known.

Now, you might be wondering why some of this info is relevant, and certainly it might not ALL be relevant to every target market in every situation. So let me break it down...

- **Location where they live**—obviously a very important one to know where to mail, and perhaps where to geo-target some of your online marketing.
- **Location where they own/invest**—if buyers, it's good to know so you can find people doing deals in the markets you want to focus on; if it's sellers, it's good to know because there might be an "out of state owner" pain point you can exploit.
- **Age**—if buyers, it's good to know because different ages might have different motivations for why they invest; if sellers, they might have different motivations for selling (such as an older audience might be looking to retire).
- **Gender**—useful for crafting messages that might be appropriate to your audience. For example, I've recently done a postcard campaign that was targeted to middle-aged women whose children were living for free in a second house. It was made even more effective because we delivered it around Mother's Day.
- **Ethnicity**—useful for crafting messages that might be appropriate to your audience. For example, perhaps your target market is from a culture that observes a certain annual celebration, then you might create marketing around that. Of course you need to be cautious here that you use ethnicity (and other factors) as a way to help you identify and communicate with your audience but not in a limiting way that racially profiles your audience negatively. (In fact, if you are using Facebook ads, you may have an additional step during the ad-building process in which you confirm that you are not using ethnicity as a limiting factor in your marketing.) That said, understanding ethnicity is helpful in marketing because you may be able to speak the native language of that people-group (for

example), so you should still consider how it applies to your marketing.

- **Religion**—useful for crafting messages that might be appropriate to your audience. For example, a lot of postcard templates say *"god bless"* on them but this might not be an appropriate thing to say if your audience does not worship God, or worships a god with a specific name, or does not believe in writing the word "god"... and many other related reasons.
- **Income**—for sellers, this helps you to understand some of their financial motivations for selling; for buyers, it can help you estimate how many deals they might do each year with you.
- **Employment**—similar to above: for sellers, this helps you to understand some of their financial motivations for selling; for buyers, it can help you estimate how many deals they might do each year with you.
- **Education**—audiences should be communicated with in a way they understand, while at the same time respecting their educational level. If you have an audience of buyers who are CFOs and MBAs and CPAs, you can communicate in a very different way than if your audience are workers who never went to college. Both could be great audiences to communicate with but their level of education will guide what you say and how you say it.
- **Marital status**—a characteristic that is useful to know the motivations of your sellers and buyers as well as their decision-making process. Motivated sellers may want to talk to a spouse before deciding to sell their house to you; cash buyers who invest for cash flow may do so because they want to spend more time with their spouse.
- **Children**—a characteristic that is useful to know the motivations of your sellers and buyers. Again, a cash buyer who invests for cash flow may love the idea of investing for cash flow so they can walk their children to school and spend more time with them in the evenings (versus missing that valuable time because they have to work at a job).
- **Hobbies/Past-times**—for sellers, this is useful to help you connect with them and remind them of what they're giving up with their stressful property; for buyers, this is useful to help you connect with them and share what they could enjoy more of through an investment with you. Targeting cash buyers who love golf may mean you can do more deals on the golf course too!
- **Level of experience with this transaction**—sellers who are new to the process might value a more educational approach versus

sellers who are familiar with selling; buyers who have invested in a lot of real estate before will value communication that is efficient and focused on ROI instead of the step-by-step stuff.

Make sense? These demographic pieces are helpful to shape your marketing and help you communicate with your audience more effectively.

Here's where to find this information: if you've done deals in the past, look at your previous deals and try to identify as many of these characteristics from the average of the people you worked with on those deals. If you have too many deals to review easily then choose the last 10-20 of your most successful deals (i.e. the most profitable or fastest or easiest or most fun) and use that information to guide you. If you've never done any deals, answer these demographic questions with your best guess of your *ideal* target market.

In many cases you'll start out with a generic "Sellers Audience Profile" and then realize that you actually have 3-4 seller target markets that you work with, even in the one city that you do deals in! That's totally fine. As you dig in, prepare to go back and create profiles for each group.

Step 2—SWOT Analysis: You've got the demographic characteristics of your target market, now it's time to go deeper. There are a few ways you can do this but I prefer the standard SWOT analysis.

SWOT stands for Strengths, Weaknesses, Opportunities, and Threats... you've probably heard of it before and it's very common in business strategy. But I like it as part of audience analysis to understand an audience and determine what the main influences are in their lives.

If you were using the SWOT analysis in your own investing business (bonus tip: you can!) you would ask:

- "What are *my* strengths?"—and you might answer that you are a rockstar sales person
- "What are *my* weaknesses?"—and you might answer that you don't like doing web design
- "What are *my* opportunities?"—and you might answer that there are a lot of motivated sellers in your city
- "What are *my* threats?"—and you might answer that there are a lot of other investors trying to do deals with those motivated sellers

Of course you can go deeper (and you should) but I just showed you that so you can see how the SWOT analysis works in your own business.

Now let's apply it to your audience: you can use this for motivated sellers that you want to work with, or cash buyers that you want to work with... or any other audience that you have. You simply answer the same questions but from their perspective.

THE REAL ESTATE INVESTING COPYWRITER'S PLAYBOOK

For example, for your motivated seller you might ask...

- "What are their strengths?"—and you might answer that they own a house with some equity
- "What are their weaknesses?"—and you might answer that they have fallen on difficult financial times and need to act quickly
- "What are their opportunities?"—and you might answer that they could keep their house, sell through an agent, list it themselves, or sell to an investor
- "What are their threats?"—and you might answer that there are less scrupulous investors than you in the market who would take advantage of them

... Again, you can go deeper but I'm just illustrating the basics for you... and the answers would be different for different types of sellers or sellers in different markets... and different for cash buyers too. For buyers, it might look like this:

- "What are their strengths?"—and you might answer that they have money
- "What are their weaknesses?"—and you might answer that they are currently investing in the stock market but not getting the returns they want
- "What are their opportunities?"—and you might answer that they could keep their current investments, invest with you, invest with a different investor, turn their money into cash, invest in Bitcoin, etc.
- "What are their threats?"—and you might answer that inflation and a desire to spend their money frivolously are threats

You'll never get the answers 100% correct; and you'll need to make some generalized assumptions for your market. That's okay. The point is to try to figure out some of the main influences in their lives... and then seek to address them in your copy, marketing, and sales process.

You'll want to leverage their strengths, help them overcome their weaknesses, position yourself as their best opportunity, and help to protect them from their weaknesses. If your marketing can achieve some or all of these things, you'll really connect with them.

SWOT is a powerful tool that isn't used a lot in audience analysis but if you try it, I think you'll see how useful it can be to reveal some of the main points you need to address in your marketing copy.

Step 3—MBTI/Phenotype: When you get into the heads of your target audience and understand what they're truly thinking and feeling, you can connect with them more effectively... you'll create more effective marketing and you'll close more deals with them too.

One of the fundamental skills in selling is building rapport with your prospects and clients, which you can do by "mirroring" their emotions, movements, and phraseology. Well, this step of identifying their MBTI/Phenotype allows you to mirror them from a distance!

The better you understand the personalities of your prospective audience, the better you will connect with them.

Consider a loud, bombastic investor with a huge ego and personality... how do you think they'd do when trying to acquire a deal from a meek and mousy seller? The seller might go along with the investor because the investor forces his way in the conversation... or they might be so frustrated and intimidated by the investor that they avoid the investor and choose to work with someone else.

Or, consider if your copy is focused on thoughts and analysis and numbers... but your audience is motivated by their feelings. Your marketing copy might not have the same impact because it does not resonate with your audience.

To solve this, you need to do your best to understand your audience's personality.

There are many different personality assessment tools out there so you can pick one that you find easy to use. Here are 3 that are really popular:

- The 4 temperaments (sanguine, choleric, melancholic, phlegmatic)
- The big 5 personalities (openness to experience, conscientiousness, extraversion, agreeableness, and neuroticism)
- Myers-Briggs (there are 16 personality combinations)

You can find more information about each of these online, or you might find one that you are familiar with and prefer instead of these. (And look, let me just add a disclaimer to say that these aren't definitive or even necessarily "Psychiatrist Approved" or completely infallible... but that's okay because we're not doing deep psycho-analysis here; we're just trying to get an overall sense of the general personality of the audience so we can write copy that the audience will more likely respond to.

The quiet, polite go-with-the-flow audiences will get the quiet, polite marketing that clearly spells out how to go with the flow; the more intense audiences will get the more direct marketing.

So, sit down and do a basic assessment of the personalities of your audience (perhaps based on some of your past clients). Then compare that assessment to your marketing copy and even your sales presentation. Do this for all audiences—for example, if you serve 2-3 different seller audiences and 2-3 different cash buyer audiences, you may need to do a personality assessment for each of them (so you'll end up with 4-6 assessments). Yes, that might seem like it will take a long time but it can dramatically increase how many deals you close so it's a great investment of your time.

Step 4—Maslow's Hierarchy: When you understand your audience's motivations, you'll uncover a virtually unlimited treasure trove of money from seller deals or from buyers' cash. When you know WHY someone does something, you can shape your marketing (and even your entire business) around the why.

In this step you'll work on understanding your audience's motivations so you can ensure your copy highlights why they should act now. This step is essential but you'll want to go through the other steps first to really understand this one.

Here's an example to illustrate why you want to know your audience's motivation: imagine a motivated seller who has a frustrating rental property with bad tenants that they can't get rid of. The seller is desperate to sell. Now imagine two investors who both approach the seller at the same time to make a cash offer on the house.

... one investor says they'll buy the house but the seller has to get rid of the tenants.

... the other investor says they'll buy the house and they'll take care of the tenants so the seller doesn't have to.

If the seller is frustrated by the tenants and doesn't even want to deal with them anymore, guess which investor they are going to go with. And they'll even accept a lower offer from the second investor just because they're motivated to avoid the hassle of dealing with those tenants.

So, how do you assess motivation? I love Maslow's hierarchy of needs. Abraham Maslow was a psychologist who developed the idea that people have an ascending order of needs, and they are motivated by these needs *in a certain order*. Their most immediate and basic needs are their own survival; their highest level needs include a sense of belonging and well-being. His hierarchy looks like this:

5. Self-actualization (feel fulfilled and purposeful)
4. Esteem (feel good about themselves)
3. Love/belonging (feel connected and social)
2. Safety needs (feel free from danger)
1. Physical needs (basic needs met, including water and food)

Maslow's hierarchy tells us that people will work to address their needs in order from lowest to highest, and we can see this as generally true in our lives: we will first make sure we have water and can eat, then we make sure we're free from danger, then we look for love and belonging, etc.

Someone might want to fall in love (a level 3 need) but they'll forget about that feeling momentarily if suddenly they find themselves in the middle of a desert. In general, people solve the lower-order needs first and once those are solved then they move to the higher-order needs.

When you try to understand the motivations of your audience, think about what is causing them to act.

For cash buyers, they might be concerned that they won't have food and drink in the future, so they'll invest now to help them in retirement; but they might also invest for other reasons too: maybe they want to spend more time with their family (love and belonging) or maybe they like to brag about their amazing cash-flow returns among friends (esteem).

For sellers, they might be trying to avoid foreclosure and barely able to pay for their family's physical needs. Once the house is foreclosed, they're worried about their family's safety. They're embarrassed by their situation (so the love/belonging need is at risk) and they are frustrated by feeling powerless against the big banks (esteem).

Those are two examples; now think about how your marketing might address those things. For sellers, chances are you've touched on some of those motivations (such as putting money in their pocket so they find a different place to live) but does your marketing talk about how you are fast and discreet so that they don't have to admit to family and friends what's happening? Or does your marketing talk about how selling to you in order to avoid foreclosure is a way for them to "stick it" to the big banks?

The deeper you go on motivations and the more thorough you are the more deals you'll do.

Step 5—Empathy Map: The final piece of the puzzle is something called an "empathy map".

An empathy map is a map of what your audience is experiencing in life:

- What they see
- What they hear
- What they think and feel
- What they say and do

And, many empathy maps also include two more components: a list of your audience's pains that they have and a list of their gains (that they would get from doing a deal with you)

You're basically getting into your audience's mind and trying to figure out all of these things as specifically as possible. For example, if you're doing an empathy map for your cash buyers, you might determine the following...

- **See:** disappointing returns from stock market investments
- **Hear:** friends who are worried about finances and the economy
- **Think and feel:** worried about their money, frustrated by lackluster returns, not sure about what to do
- **What they say and do:** they may make bigger bets on riskier investments or they might tuck their money under their mattress
- **Pain:** they're worried about going to zero and going broke
- **Gain:** when they do a deal with you, they have consistent returns

This is a very simplified example but it's just meant to show you how to use these. You'll want to go as deep as possible and get as specific as possible. Think back to previous deals to remember the specific things that your audience as said or done. For example, maybe a seller going through foreclosure was prompted to call you because they got another reminder letter from the bank... so that's something you'd put under "see". Or maybe a seller whose house is in probate is frustrated by the heirs who are all fighting over what to do with the house... so that might go in "hear".

Summary

Want a strong start to your marketing? It starts with understanding your audience and getting into their brain to know how that person thinks and feels.

Without fail, the clients who come to me with a crystal clear sense of what their customers say and do are the ones who are able to get the most effective copy from me and are also the ones who grow their businesses the fastest.

Get to know your audience! Use this 5-step audience profiling strategy for every audience you want to work with, and try to get as specific as possible to understand them.

BONUS: Get a worksheet for this chapter at:
RealEstateInvestingCopywriter.com/bonus/playbookbonus

CHAPTER 3: WIIFM+ROI=$$$

What's the purpose of all marketing and sales? It's to get the other person (your audience) to take action. For those of us who are real estate investors, that action is usually to get a seller to sell their house to us or to get buyers to invest their money with us.

(Of course there might be other actions that you want someone to take, depending on the kind of investing you do—maybe you flip houses and sell to retail buyers; maybe you do vacation rentals so you're trying to connect with vacationers; maybe you do rent-to-owns so you're marketing to tenant-buyers; the list goes on and on.)

Action is key here. If you're not trying to get your audience to take action, don't bother marketing.

No matter who you are trying to connect with, and what you want them to do, the way that you can compel them to take action is to follow the two immutable rules of marketing, which I'll illustrate with this simple scenario: imagine that you're a single person who is enjoying the dating scene, you're not in a serious relationship, and you have no dependents. Well, one day you're cruising down the street in your car when you drive past a billboard for... *diapers*.

Do you care? Probably not. There is no child in your life and none appearing anytime soon in your life so your subconscious tunes out the ad.

But what if the ad was for a cologne or perfume that says, *"you'll attract more desirable people when wearing this scent"*?

You've just encountered two of the most important rules for all of marketing and sales. In this chapter we'll look at these two immutable rules of marketing. If you keep these two things in mind every time you create marketing material for your investing company, and every time you sit down with a seller or buyer to work with them face-to-face, you'll get far in the world of investing.

These rules are expressed as two acronyms, which you may have encountered before: **WIIFM** and **ROI**.

Although their meanings overlap a bit, I like to consider both at the same time because there are differences.

Rule #1: WIIFM

WIIFM stands for "What's In It For Me?"

People are busy, they have limited time and attention, and they are selfish. Simply put, none of us can pay attention to everything all the time. We only have a limited amount of focus to give to anything. Therefore, if you want your marketing to receive any attention at all, you need to tell your audience what's in it for them.

You just read the example earlier where you see an advertisement for diapers. But if you are someone with no baby in your life, and perhaps no plan for one in the near future, the advertising for diapers does not matter to you at all. It was only the cologne/perfume advertisement that mattered to you so you paid attention to it.

The lesson here is: all of your marketing needs to express a specific message to the right audience—a message about why it's important for them to pay attention to you.

Often, marketing efforts don't really focus on the WIIFM and instead just reports the facts. An advertisement that says, "this car has 4 doors" is just a dry fact and not really an effective ad; however, if the advertisement says, "this car has 4 doors, which means that you can put your children in the backseat easily" does a better job of explaining why a fact matters.

SHORTCUT

When writing your marketing copy, list out the features of whatever you're selling and then after each feature add the words, "this means you can..."

So, for sellers you might say, "sell your house to me in 7 days" (which is the feature) and then add the words "this means you can..." afterward to force yourself to consider why it's important to them. You'll end up with something like: "Sell your house to me in 7 days. This means you can be rid of the hassles and headaches of owning that house fast."

And, for buyers you might say, "invest for 20% returns" (which is the feature) and then add the words "this means you can..." afterward to force yourself to consider why it's important to them. You'll end up with something like: "Invest for 20% returns. This means you can quit your job and retire early, while enjoying passive cash flow that replaces your income. Spend more time on the golf course!"

If you have done your research to develop your audience in the previous chapter then making sure that all your marketing addresses the WIIFM rule will be simple.

Rule #2: ROI

ROI stands for Return On Investment. You are probably familiar with the concept as an investor—you invest in a property and expect to get a return on that investment of more money than what you invested.

The concept of ROI isn't limited to just investors. Consider that every purchase anyone makes is an investment of money, time, and effort, and someone wants to know that they will get *some kind of* ROI on that purchase. (For example, a burger at McDonald's has an ROI of taste and convenience for some people.) Your sellers and buyers will need to know the ROI for them when they respond to your marketing.

People are busy and they don't have unlimited resources of time or money. They don't have time to try everything, nor do they have the financial resources to buy everything. They need to decide if any given decision is right for them to spend their limited resources on.

You just read the example earlier where the ad for perfume or cologne suggested that you'd meet more desirable people when wearing that scent. Purchasing cologne or perfume is a cost but if the ad shows that there is a return on that investment (the *investment* being the purchase of the perfume or cologne, and the *return* being that you'll have beautiful people flocking to you) then the ad is showing that you get something back in exchange for your purchase.

The lesson here is: all of your marketing needs to show that your audience will benefit to a greater perceived degree than the perceived cost of the action.

And it's not just money we're talking about, either! Any decision that your audience makes is an investment of assets (like money, time, effort, peace-of-mind, reputation, and more) and they hope that the purchase provides a greater amount of return than the combined "cost" of those assets.

One example might be: if a motivated seller is facing financial difficulty and worried that their house will be foreclosed on (and worried that his or her neighbors will find out about the financial challenges), then the assets at stake are money (because of the foreclosure) and reputation (because of the thought of what the neighbors will think).

If you come in as an investor and make an offer on their house, they might feel that the money they're getting from you isn't as much as they could get if they sold the house through a real estate agent; however, they are able to sell fast, save a ton of hassle, and most importantly, avoid the embarrassment that they're worried about. So, you're asking them to make a decision that involves giving up some of the money they were hoping to get on the house (that's the "investment" side of the decision) but in return you are giving them something they value even more (the return on the investment, which is a preserved reputation).

If you've done the research to understand your target audience then you will probably be aware of what investments you're asking each audience to make and what returns you're providing them.

To help you, here is a list of resources that people have that they are looking to invest or protect or get a return of:

- Money
- Time
- Reputation
- Pride
- Comfort
- Effort
- Focus/Attention
- Happiness
- Peace-of-mind (as opposed to stress)
- Credit rating
- Spending time with family
- Lifestyle
- Safety
- Care and protection of family

How To Use WIIFM And ROI Effectively

When marketing to sellers and buyers, you may find that your marketing or sales efforts do not result in a deal. Maybe the seller doesn't respond to your postcard, or when meeting face-to-face they don't agree to sell their house to you. Or, maybe the buyer doesn't take action when presented with a great deal, or they seemed interested but just don't wire their money to you so you can send them the deal.

This WILL happen at some point in your marketing and sales efforts. When it does, come back to this chapter and dig in further and try to add more WIIFM and ROI to all of your marketing and sales efforts.

You can never add enough. When you think you've added enough, keep going. And if you don't get anyone taking action, add even more. Stack it high with every WIIFM reason and every possible ROI that you can think of.

The more you know about your target audience, the better you'll be at stacking these up. And remember: just become someone is a seller doesn't mean they value the same WIIFM and ROI as other sellers. You might have more than one target audience (for example, you might be working with two different kinds of sellers, such as those going through foreclosure as well as burnt-out landlords). In those cases, each type of seller will value different WIIFM and ROI factors. The person going through foreclosure might be worried about their reputation and getting back to "normal" while the burnt-out landlord might just want to reduce stress and spend more time with their family.

You cannot stack too many WIIFM and ROI factors. Of course that may not mean that you present all of them in every piece of marketing but it's important to think about which ones apply to each audience.

When creating your marketing, put the biggest factors front and center so they are the primary ones that your target audience sees. Then, you can always add the other ones in later (further down in the same marketing piece, if appropriate, or in different marketing pieces… or just keep them in your back pocket to pull out when you need to really convince them to work with you).

PRO TIP

Sometimes you'll work with sellers or buyers who have more than one decision-maker present. For example:

- A retired seller who wants to sell as-is might have their adult child there to help them navigate the transaction
- A seller in financial distress will probably have their spouse at the dining room table when you are talking
- A cash flow investor may have a business partner listen to you pitch your opportunity too

When this happens, remember that everyone has different WIIFM and ROI considerations—even the decision-makers whose names may not appear in the transaction! You will be more effective when you prepare for their WIIFM and ROI considerations as well.

CHAPTER 4: COMPETITION

I connected with a prospective client on the phone recently. He'd reached out to me through my website and set up a call, and now we were meeting to see if I could help him.

One of the first things he told me was the reason why he'd sought me out in the first place: he was in a highly competitive market and he discovered by accident that he was sending exactly the same postcards as other investors... several investors.

(Apparently, a seller called the investor and said, "I am holding three postcards in my hands—one from you and two from other people—and they say exactly the same thing. And, these aren't the first ones I received this week.")

The investor started to realize that the money he was spending on postcards was being wasted because his target audience of motivated sellers was opening the mailbox and pulling out potentially up to a dozen nearly-identical postcards from their mail box.

Almost all of the postcards looked and sounded the same: they used a punchy headline, personalization, and the offer to buy the seller's house for cash. Oh, and they were all on bright yellow or bright pink paper.

Realizing that he needed to send something different, he went in search for a copywriter who knew something about real estate investing... and that's how he ended up meeting with me.

It's not surprising that he reached out after discovering just how competitive his market is. That's one of the top reasons why investors get in touch with me: because they learn that their postcards (or yellow letters or other forms of marketing) that they bought as a template from a guru turn out to be used by *everyone*. So they seek out someone like me who can give them unique copy that is highly targeted and far more effective than the generic boilerplate copy that every other competitor is sending.

As an investor, you will face many different kinds of competition when marketing to sellers *and* when marketing to buyers. After all, sellers have just one house and buyers have a finite amount of money to invest, and you probably aren't the only one who wants that property or that capital.

And there's a further problem: whether or not you have a lot of competing investors in your market, you probably have a bigger competitor problem than you realize. In fact, most investors do.

You see, your competition is made up of three different types of competitors:

1. Direct competitors
2. Indirect competitors
3. Inaction

To illustrate the difference in a simple way, consider the need people have to get around your city. If you own a car dealership then your direct competition is other car dealerships; your indirect competition include buses, taxis, and bicycles; and the competition of inaction is your prospective car buyer just staying home and not bothering to go anywhere.

Of course that's a simple example but the principle is true for us in the real estate investing industry: whether or not you realize it, you face each one of these three types of competition in your investing business. Fortunately, each of these can be addressed and countered with copywriting and marketing strategies, which we'll look at below.

In this chapter we'll take a deeper-dive into the different types of competitors and then you'll learn a number of practical strategies to out-compete.

A Deep-Dive Into The Different Types Of Competitors

First, let's look at your competition. You should get a piece of paper and make a list of the types of competitors that you face (depending on the type of investing you do). Later in this chapter you'll use this list as a checklist to make sure that the strategies you deploy can help you compete against each of the competitors on your list.

Below are the three types of competitors. (Brace yourself, I'm sharing some harsh truths I've learned about investors in the years I've worked with them… some of these insights may hit too close to home and force you to rethink how you compete in your market).

Direct competitors: In a discussion about competition, your direct competitors are the most obvious ones. These are other investors who are just like you. They likely introduce themselves in the same way to sellers or buyers, they probably make the same offer to sellers or buyers, and they probably provide the same services as you.

For example, when you're working with sellers, your direct competitors are the other investors who are trying to buy the property. When working with buyers, your direct competitors are the other investors who are trying to get that buyer's capital.

(Clarification: some real estate investors will have read that above paragraph and will have the rebuttal, "but no one serves the seller or buyer as well as I do; they simply don't have all the connections and resources that I do. Unfortunately, that is rarely as true as you think it is; many investors have services that are as good as yours. And look at it from the sellers' and buyers' perspective: when faced with two investors who are each claiming to have the best options for them, those sellers and buyers don't know. Investors can look identical even if they are not.)

This competition exists for the one simple reason that you are also in business: because there is an opportunity in the market that needs a solution.

Indirect competitors: While your direct competitors are those who are just like you, your indirect competitors are those who offer a similar solution to sellers or buyers but whose solution is different from yours.

For example, when working with motivated sellers, your indirect competition might include real estate agents or For Sale By Owner products and services. Or, when working with buyers, your indirect competition might include real estate agents (who can help them buy properties) or even the stock market where they can park their capital.

(Clarification: as soon as you read that above paragraph, some investors might again react negatively to what I'm saying because they believe their services are superior to real estate agents' services or the returns provided by the stock market. While that may be true, think of it from the prospective sellers' or buyers' perspectives who don't immediately see the difference between you and your indirect competitor. To them, it's just a different way to solve their problem.)

This competition exists because there can be multiple ways to solve problems, just as you read earlier when I gave the example of a bus, bicycle, or taxi as indirect competition to the purchase of a car from a car dealership. The solution from an indirect competitor will often look very different than your solution, even if the outcome (from the sellers' or buyers' perspectives) seems to be the same.

The competition of inaction: Your "competition of inaction" is a third option that sellers and buyers have. That is, they can simply choose to do nothing. Therefore, as an investor, you are competing again inaction.

For example, when working with motivated sellers, a burnt-out landlord might look at your postcard offering them to buy but they may choose to do nothing because it seems easier. Or, when working with buyers, they may see a great cash-flowing property but they choose not to act because it seems easier to do nothing.

This competition exists because people have an innate desire for stasis, even if it's painful. That is: the temporary emotional pain that a burnt out landlord feels when dealing with his or her tenants is still less than the perceived pain of how complicated it could be to sell the property.

Here Are The Strategies To Out-Compete Your Competition

We've looked at each type of competition you face and why they exist. Now it's time to look at strategies that can help you out-compete your competition.

#1. In some situations, *wait, and follow-up strategically*. Yeah, this one sounds weird and it definitely doesn't work in every situation, so let me explain: in some markets (especially larger markets), you end up getting a bunch of those high priced gurus coming to town who put on a free or low-cost investing event. After the event, thousands of newbie investors send out postcards to the market but don't have their follow-through dialed in, and many can't figure out what to do if and when a seller follows up on a postcard. So, just wait. Let the market be flooded with offers from newbie investors who can't follow-through. Then, you should follow-up because 99.9% of those newbie investors will have left the market but they'll have softened up the sellers who are looking to sell. Follow-up with professionalism and a plan, and you can scoop up the sellers who are not being served by those here-one-day-gone-the-next investors.

#2. Care. Another powerful competition-busting strategy is the ability to empathize with, and care for, your prospective sellers and buyers. There are many investors in the industry who are just in it for the money and their flashy, bombastic approach might get peoples' attention but it won't keep them. If you can demonstrate to sellers and to buyers that you care, you'll win against other investors who don't provide the same human connection. Of course the key here is to *show* you care. You can't just tell yourself that you care more, and you can't just say you care; you have to actually show it in your words and actions. The simplest and fastest way to show you care is to double the number of questions you ask, and listen twice as much too.

#3. Build relationships. I'm not just talking about building relationships with sellers and buyers. After all, if you care (see #2, above) then you automatically will anyway. I'm talking about relationships with other people—other investors, real estate agents, contractors, accountants, attorneys, etc. These are referral relationships because you can refer clients to them (or they can refer them to you). Invest your time heavily in relationship-building and you'll build a really strong, long-lasting business that can handle the ups and downs of the market.

SHORT CUT

Want the fastest way to build relationships? Do this: Make a big list of the professionals that you want to have a relationship with. Then talk to two of them every single day, without fail. (If you call one and they're not there, leave a message and keep dialing or visiting the people on your list until you talk to two people). Do it every single day. It should take less than 30 minutes to introduce yourself to two people each day and ask how you can help them. And if you put in just 30 minutes (or less) on this activity every day, you'll have established relationships with 730 potential referral partners.

Of course don't just introduce yourself once and never follow-up. Build a relationship. It costs nothing but time (and maybe a few bucks in stamps to send a letter or even lunch for the really promising referral partners). Think about how you can help them by sending referrals or helping them in some other way.

While your competitors are going broke fighting with each other over just a few sellers that they acquire with postcards, you can build a deep book of referrals who can send you sellers and buyers that would never receive or respond to your competitors' typical marketing.

#4. Specialize. I'll talk about this a bit more in an upcoming chapter but you'll want to seriously think about specializing. You see, many investors just serve a general market of *any* motivated seller and *any* cash buyer, and that might work for some but it's hard to target those large, vague audiences with effective copy, and it's hard to set yourself apart from all the other generalist investors out there. The secret is to specialize. Find a market that you connect with really well and specialize in them. You'll build marketing that resonates more effectively and you'll have higher credibility because of it.

#5. Differentiate. Another way to fight against your competitors is by differentiating yourself in some way. Your direct competition are all fighting as generalists and that makes them forgettable. However, if you can identify a way to be different than everyone else, do it. A simple way to differentiate might be to leverage something you've done in your past. If you were a military veteran, MMA cage fighter, Olympian, or failed business owner, build your marketing around that. (Incidentally, I've done just that for those 4 investors). If you are a little old lady who also knows Kung-Fu, build your marketing around that. If you were once a chef, build your marketing around that. When you speak and act differently than everyone else, you become memorable and stand out.

#6. Productize your solutions. Most investors have a variety of strategies that will allow them to help their sellers or buyers. Perhaps you buy properties that you plan to flip, and you have several financial "tools" in your toolbox that give you several options to buy properties. Or maybe you work with cash buyers and have a number of investing strategies, depending on their financial goals and timelines. A lot of investors have access to these solutions but they don't use them in a competitive way. One fast, powerful way to become more competitive in your market is to turn your standard solutions into products. You don't have to make any changes to the solution than to simply give it a name. So, for example, if you work with sellers and you can either buy their house for cash now OR offer them the option to hold a note on the house, then simply turn it into two options with names like: "The Cash Today Solution™" for sellers who want to get cash now, and the "ValuePlus Income Stream Solution™" for sellers who are willing to accept payments over time. To productize, simply list out all the ways that you help your sellers and buyers and then give that solution a benefits-oriented name that highlights what's in it for the seller or buyer.

SHORT CUT

Here's a simple way to make even more powerful product names: If you know the keywords that you want to target in search engines, use that as a starting point for your product name. For example, if you are an investor in Phoenix Arizona and you're targeting the keyword "Sell My House Fast Phoenix" then make your productized solution the "Sell My House Fast Phoenix Solution™".

This is a powerful way to compete with direct competitors because it makes your solution seem clearer and better thought out than a competitor who just says "we have lots of ways we can help."

#7. Enhance your credibility. Credibility is a social "credit" that you get from prospective sellers or buyers based on how authentic and authoritative they believe you to be. Credibility is achieved through how clearly you communicate, how knowledgeable you appear, how carefully targeted your solutions are, and your collection of proven case studies and testimonials that you have. (There are other factors that can contribute to credibility but those are four very powerful factors and if you focus on building those, you'll appear very credible to your sellers and buyers.)

One quick note about credibility: in most cases, credibility doesn't work *on its own* as the only strategy to out-compete your competitors. Credibility is important but in my experience, it is most effective when you combine it with some of the other strategies mentioned here. That's because it compounds the effectiveness of whatever you are highlighting but if you are a generalist who is trying to be more credible, you simply highlight how much of a generalist you are. But if you are a well-differentiated specialist who builds relationships, adding credibility on top of that can really make it work.

#8. Education. Like credibility, above, education is another enhancer that can compound some of the other competitive strategies in this list. When you educate your sellers and buyers, you make yourself the knowledgeable expert, and people tend to follow experts and do what they instruct. Create educational material around every aspect of the transaction and present it in an attractive format. Even if you do exactly the same thing as every other competitor, the winning competitor is the one who will walk the seller or buyer step-by-step through the process. The trick is not to overwhelm the seller or buyer in the beginning with all of your education but rather to simply show that you have it, and to reveal it in piece as you build rapport with them. Consider using education pieces like checklists, assessments, mini reports, and even books. (Even if the seller or buyer never reads any of it, the presence of this educational material, and the sheer volume of it, can help to convince a seller or buyer that you are the right person to do business with.)

#9. Step-by-step checklist. This strategy is specifically designed to help you overcome the competition of inaction that you might face with sellers and buyers in your market. The strategy is: to create a one-page numbered checklist with each step of the process clearly outlined and a simple, clear step should be listed. The seller or buyer should be able to go through the list and complete each step in the sequence to complete their goal (whatever goal they happen to have—such as selling their house fast for cash, buying a cash-flowing property, or something else). The underlying concept is that people have a tendency to want to complete things that they start, especially if the steps are clear and simple. Conversely, people get stalled when they don't know what to do or when the steps are difficult. This checklist should help to solve that. It would be even more effective if you work with them to check off the first 2-3 check boxes even before you put the house under contract. That will help them feel like they are making progress even before they make their selling or buying decision.

Summary

Investors face stiff competition and must bring to bear all of the tools and strategies and resources they possibly can in order to compete. The greater the level of competition you face in your market (from all three types of competition) the more you need to build so you can rise above your competition.

Keep reading because many of the strategies you'll learn in this book will show you really practical ways to overtake your competition.

Ultimately, remember this: competition is not bad. In fact, you should welcome it. Even though it can have the effect of raising the purchase price of properties or lowering the sale price, it can also help us to streamline our sales process so we get laser-focused on helping sellers and buyers. It also prepares us—because there will always be some form of competition and if we are ready for it then we can handle more competition if and when it happens.

PRO TIP

Never ever speak negatively about your completion. Always, always, always take the high road. Even if your competitors are unethical, you will not do yourself any favors by telling the sellers or buyers about them. After all, if your competitor is unethical to your seller or buyer, what's to stop your competitor from slandering you unethically as well?

Your best approach is to educate your seller or buyer and give them tools to help make a better decision. For example, if you are working with cash buyers and they mention a competitor who you know lies about his or her experience as an investor then the better approach is to teach your buyer about how to tell the difference between an experienced investor and an inexperienced one.

BONUS: I've created bunch of resources and downloadables for you here: RealEstateInvestingCopywriter.com/bonus/playbookbonus

Use these to dig deeper into the chapters and apply each chapters' lessons to your investing business.

This is what I always tell investors…

PART 2: YOUR BRAND

The competition is fierce. Sellers and buyers have many choices available to them—from other investors… to other ways to sell or buy… even to the choice of doing nothing!

You may be the very best option for them but simply *being* the best isn't enough to get those sellers to do business with you. You need to communicate why you are the best, and you need to communicate it in a way that connects with your audience so they understand and value you.

This part builds upon what you learned in Part 1. By the end of Part 2 you'll have a really strong, compelling brand (or more than one, depending on your business) hat you'll proudly use to help you do more deals.

CHAPTER 5: SPECIALIZATION AND DIFFERENTIATION

When I talk to real estate investors, one of the biggest problems I hear from them is: "the competition in my market is brutal." (As someone who talks to investors *all over the US*, I hear this everywhere. And yeah, there are some hotspots where it's particularly bad but many investors feel the crush of competition. You're not alone. That's why I wrote this book.)

Why Is There So Much Competition?

Well, it's complex but part of the problem is that many other people are becoming investors perhaps for the same reasons that you became an investor: They were probably attracted to the cash flow or the ability to change the financial game for you and your family. And there are others (you've probably met many of them) who saw all the money being made on those real estate flipping television shows and wanted in on that.

And another part of the problem is that *anyone* can become a real estate investor. In my opinion, that's actually one of the great things about investing—it's so simple to get started. But it also means that anyone who wants to can get into it.

And a third part of the problem is that many experts go on to help other people become real estate investors (and I confess that many of those experts are using *my* copywriting and marketing to do turn more people into investors—sorry about that!). There are many experts empowering more people to become investors.

And a fourth part of the problem is that today's rapidly advancing technology allows people to become investors from anywhere. Heck, I wholesaled deals in other parts of the US and I help many investors who do deals in other areas.

Therefore, in an area that might have had just a small handful of investors in the past, there are now many investors who can overwhelm the mailboxes of motivated sellers with similar looking postcards. And it just gets worse whenever one of those as-seen-on-TV investing gurus waltzes through town with their how-to-get-rich-in-real-estate seminars. Suddenly, hundreds of people attend their pitch-fest and feel fully qualified to do deals, then flood the market with direct mail.

It Gets Worse...

I've only just described the cause of the problem, not the actual problem itself. The *cause* of the problem is that many, many people jump into real estate investing (and there's a long line of people behind them who will become real estate investors very soon).

But the *actual* problem is: motivated sellers and cash buyers (or whomever you are trying to reach with your marketing) become overwhelmed with similar offers from a thousand people who all sound the same.

Let's say you send out one of those "Yellow Letters." Perhaps like a lot of my clients, they might have worked a few years ago but now they don't work as much... or even at all. And the reason? Because your Yellow Letter is not the only Yellow Letter in the mailbox.

Neither is that "Third Notice" postcard that everyone loves to send.

They were good for a long time but you've probably seen response rates declining from them. It's not necessarily because the copy is old; it's often because the seller has seen dozens of the same postcard every month.

And, when a motivated seller calls from a bandit sign, or a cash buyer meets another investor at a local REIA, or when either of these people seek out an investor online, what do they find? Probably the same thing: an army of nearly-cloned investors who are offering exactly the same thing.

Here's the honest truth that you may not want to know: chances are, the seller and the buyer can't tell the difference between you and the 10 or 30 or 50 other real estate investors in the market. Everyone is trying to get their attention.

(Now, a bunch of readers may get to this point and angrily object to what I've just written by saying: "but I'm different!" Fair enough. Maybe you are the rare exception. But a lot of investors aren't different from each other and to an uneducated seller or buyer, they can't tell that you are different. The onus is on you to explain how you're different.)

Go to your fridge and pull out a carton of eggs and take a look at them. If you want to have bacon and eggs, which egg is the one you want to eat? Yeah, each one looks exactly identical and it almost makes no difference at all which one you choose. Sure, there might be subtle differences in the egg... in the color texture of the shell or even in the flavor of the egg... but you don't have an expert eye because you're not an insider in the egg industry. You just randomly grab one egg because it looks a lot like the other 11 in the carton, and you eat it with your bacon and you're happy because you got what you wanted.

The motivated seller and the cash buyer experience the same thing. In the town of Smithville, the motivated seller can't see the difference between Smithville Home Buyers, We Buy Houses Smithville LLC, and JunkHouses4CashSmithville.com. They all seem the same to the motivated seller (and similar thing happens on the buyer side as well).

So, some will choose you and many will choose one of the other investing companies because they can't tell the difference.

But it's not all bad news. There is a solution…

Here's The Solution

If no one can tell you apart, how do you expect to get any business? Fortunately, there's a simple solution. And for the people who adopt this solution, it's simple, fun, and very, very effective.

All you need to do is separate yourself from the pack: just find a way to *differentiate* yourself so that you can rise above the noise.

You do that with something I call a "Point Of Difference." A Point Of Difference is something that sets you apart from every other real estate investor in your market. It's the aspect of your business that makes you unique, compared to all the other investing companies out there.

A Point Of Difference is an angle or approach that sets you apart from other investors. It makes you unique in your market. Your Point Of Difference should be built around something that, when people hear it, they think of you (or when people hear you, they think of it).

When you differentiate, you set yourself apart, which means you end up in some of the same mailboxes as other investors but your marketing looks different so you will rise to the top of the stack of mail—that will make you stand out from the crowd and, if your Point Of Difference is effective, it will also prompt sellers and buyers to want to work with you.

If you have a background in marketing, perhaps you've heard of a related concept called a "USP" or "Unique Selling Proposition." A USP is similar but focused around one key benefit of a product or service. What I'm talking about here may be similar but doesn't have to be: Your Point Of Difference could be an aspect of your service or it could be a unique story about you or even a funny, crazy, or memorable thing you do.

Very briefly, here are some examples of various Points of Difference:

- Maybe you have a unique hobby or career—as is the case of one of my clients who was a Navy SeaBee, another client was a former Olympic champion, and another client who was an MMA Cage Fighter.

- Maybe you have an interesting story—as was the case of several clients who grew up in poverty and harsh conditions but went on to become extremely wealthy and successful, or even one client was wounded in Afghanistan (*by friendly fire!*) yet rose above his challenges to become an investor.
- Maybe you specialize in buying specific types of houses. One of my clients buys houses just from seniors who want to extract their equity and move into a retirement home, or maybe you only buy houses that have mold. That will obviously appeal to a certain group of motivated sellers. And on the buyer side, maybe you have the largest selection of rent-to-own homes in a school district. Clearly that is something that will appeal to buyers.
- Maybe you have a cultural and ethnic background that allows you to interact well with a certain group of people—for example maybe you are of Chinese descent and you speak Mandarin fluently. You can leverage that into your Point Of Differentiation quite effectively.

There are many more possibilities, too, but these are a good start. Choose just one or two and construct them into a Point Of Differentiation for you.

Suddenly, even if thousands of other people are sending out "Third Notice" postcards to your market, your marketing can rise to the top of those sellers' mailboxes because yours say: "I'm A Black Belt In Karate And I'll Kick Your House Problems To The Curb" (and of course show a picture of you with your Black Belt). And then invite them to "Call My Dojo at 555-BELT to make a lightning fast cash offer."

And here's the power of this: maybe the prospective seller doesn't need your service right now. Or a month from now.

But you keep sending postcards. And every one of them has a picture of you and a little marketing message about your Black Belt in Karate. And a few months down the road, maybe they do need to sell their house. Well, who are they going to remember? A hundred other investors who sent them "Third Notice" postcards that were identical? Or the Black Belt guy with the memorable phone number?

Investors Love This Idea But Get Scared To Do It

While this sounds good in practice, it's actually hard for some investors to identify their Point Of Difference. The reason is: they think that by differentiating themselves, they are limiting who they can work with, and therefore will lose out on some amazing deals. Well yes, you will limit who you work with and you will lose out on some deals… but in my experience, you end up getting more deals because you suddenly become much more memorable and attractive to the right people.

Investors who reject the idea of this Point Of Differentiation think that they'd rather have a small slice of a big pie (that is: the chance to get a few of the deals even though they're up against a lot of competition).

Except that's not what happens. What really happens is: you end up with a slice so small it's microscopic because there are just SO MANY more people trying the same thing.

How To Create Your Point Of Differentiation

There are several ways to create your Point Of Differentiation, and I've shown you a few above. There are many others—including who your target market is, what kind of houses you sell or buy, or a skill you might have.

For example: I've helped a few investors focus in on marketing to people who own a second home with a freeloading family member living in that house. Our marketing didn't just target absentee owners; it targeted absentee owners with a very specific problem… it just happened to be a common problem, but one that no one else was addressing.

Or here's an example to show that your Point Of Differentiation doesn't have to be serious, and it doesn't have to have anything to do with your business. For example, if you have a cute dog then pretend that it's the dog that is buying the houses and all of your marketing comes from the dog. It's silly but incredibly memorable. (Your sellers will actually look forward to getting postcards "from" that dog in the mail… and they'll insist that you bring the dog with you when you meet them.)

In order to create your point of differentiation, you just need to answer one question: "***What can I do or say that absolutely no one else in my market is doing or saying right now?***" Answer that question and you probably have your point of differentiation.

Now that you've read the question, it's harder than you were expecting, right? I meet a lot of investors who think they have a Point Of Differentiation in their business but when I ask them what it is, they say, "we have a lot of financial tools to help a motivated seller," or, "we have a great inventory of wholesale deals under contract for cash buyers."

Ummmm… sorry, that's not unique. Chances are, you don't have any more financial tools to help motivated sellers compared to a dozen other investors who are claiming the same thing. Chances are, you don't have any more inventory than a dozen other wholesalers who are claiming the same thing. And even if you do, there are other investors probably claiming the same thing. Besides, it's not attention-getting, it's not memorable, and the seller or buyer doesn't care. Pick something that will get the prospective seller's or buyer's attention.

(Interesting side note: I used to write for real estate agents and I saw this a lot then too. Many agents would proudly proclaim that they'd sell someone's house with as much care and attention as they'd sell their own. They thought that was their Point Of Differentiation... even though a dozen or more real estate agents were saying exactly the same thing! So investors are not alone in the need to create a Point Of Differentiation.)

Often, I see investors who are differentiating in the following not-very-unique ways...

- By promising great service (what is that and how is it better than someone else's? And does a motivated seller really want service? No they don't!)
- By talking about how quickly they can act (can you close in week? Most investors can!)
- By promising to give the fairest price or the highest cash offer they can (although the wording is fuzzy in order to maintain compliance)

When more than one person says it, it's not unique. The only way to truly differentiate is to find something that no one else does or says.

If possible, it should be something that no one else does—like if you are a Navy SEAL, or you speak a language that your audience speaks, or you pretend it's your dog who is buying the houses. That's the best way to differentiate and make sure your competition can't touch you.

Look at your processes, your sales funnel, your skills, your team, your network of people, your experience, and anything that is unique or even silly about you, and incorporate that into your differentiation.

However, if you are struggling, or if you want a REALLY fast start in differentiation, then there is another way...

If necessary, it could be something that no one else says they do. Here's a famous marketing story to illustrate: the Lucky Strike cigarette company was trying to differentiate their marketing against all the other cigarette brands out there. A marketer looked at their process and told them to add the words, "Our tobacco is toasted!" to their packaging. Lucky Strike balked at this because all tobacco in every cigarette made (even made by the competition) is toasted before it's turned into a cigarette. However, the marketer pointed out that no one else was *saying* it. Lucky Strike did just that in 1917 and it was a transformational marketing campaign for them.

If you are struggling to find a way to differentiate your investing company against the many others in your market, try to find the "toasted" aspect of your company. The key is: no one else should be saying it (so "we offer great service" when many other investors are saying the same thing is not the right approach).

> ### SHORT CUT
>
> **There's an even faster way to differentiate**: There's another way to use this "it's toasted" method very successfully and I've done this with a lot of my clients who truly have businesses that look nearly identical to their competition. When we can't differentiate by something they *do*, and when we can't find something in their business to *say* that they do as a Point Of Differentiation, then do this very simple yet very powerful strategy…
>
> Figure out what's important to your audience (a seller or a buyer or whatever) and then list that part of the process out step-by-step… and then create a name for those steps, and then add the letters TM after it.
>
> For example, if you have motivated sellers who want to move in a hurry, then pull together the processes that you would use and brand it as the "QuickMove Strategy™". Then make sure all your marketing boasted about "Call us for an appointment and we'll not only give you a fast cash offer, we'll make sure you get our Platinum QuickMove Strategy™ for free!"
>
> That "QuickMove Strategy" could be a completely normal and average service that every investor offers to every seller but if you make it into a simple checklist or flowchart and give it a name like that, you can create a simple Point Of Differentiation that can appear on every piece of marketing you send out. Use this sparingly, though. I once worked with an investor and I did this once for the main point of differentiation and later I happened to check in on his business and he had done this for many different pieces of his business and it lost the effect.
>
> This is a very simple yet powerful way to differentiate, and it's fast too. So it's a good way to get started if you are new to investing or if you are still trying to decide if there is a stronger point of differentiation that you can use.

Now That You Have Your Point Of Differentiation… What's Next?

Just identifying your Point Of Differentiation isn't enough. Now you need to actually do something with it. And what should you do with it?

Put it EVERYWHERE.

Your Point Of Differentiation should be everywhere. And when you think "oh, that's too much"… then you're halfway there and you should find other places to put it.

When it comes to differentiation, subtlety and humility are not the answers. Frankly, you need to club people over the head with your point of differentiation.

For example, if you're the Navy SEAL I mentioned earlier...

- You need to have pictures of you in your uniform on every marketing piece.
- Your marketing needs to be headlined with words like: "What does this Navy SEAL want to do with your house?"
- Your website needs to be something like: sealbuyshouses.com or something like that.
- All your marketing should have a small piece of camouflage coloring on it.
- Your brand should be reminiscent of a military logo.
- Your process should be labelled with something that feels SEAL-like, such as: "Get our FastStrike Cash Offer™".

Or, If you're using the QuickMove™ Strategy...

- You need to have an image of the checklist or flowchart and put it on everything.
- Your marketing needs to say something like: "We're the developer of the QuickMove™ Strategy" on nearly every piece of marketing you send out.
- The back of your business card should say, "ask me about our QuickMove™ Strategy."
- And you should write a book called exactly that—*The QuickMove™ Strategy For Homeowners*.

Your Point Of Differentiation should be everywhere on everything and you should bring it up in conversation with prospects regularly.

How much should you share it? Well, let me put it this way: imagine you're the investor who markets "*my dog buys houses.*" One day you stop at the grocery store to pick up some groceries. While you're at the register, the cashier sees you and exclaims: "Oh! You're the guy whose dog buys houses. Where's your dog, is he buying your groceries too?" It's funny but it's a great measure of how successful your Point Of Differentiation is.

When random people stop you because they recognize your marketing, that's when you know you have finally differentiated enough and shared it effectively.

And once you know what your Point Of Differentiation is (as well as your avatar and your sales funnel), you'll probably find that you start to get more calls because your marketing stands out more in the mailboxes and minds of the people you want to reach. You may capture their attention in a full mailbox, or you may even move strategically into the mailboxes and minds that no one else is reaching right now.

Summary

The competition may seem rough right now but that's only because you appear to be too much like your competitors. There is a very simple solution to that: eliminate the competition by becoming a category of one.

Set yourself apart with a powerful Point of Differentiation that no one else is doing or saying in your marketplace right now.

Find a point of differentiation for your business, or for every audience you have (probably a seller audience and a buyer audience) and make sure that you share that differentiation everywhere.

Does it feel like a risk? Sure it does. But the greater risk is NOT doing it and hoping that your cloned postcard finds its way into the right hands. It's counterintuitively less of a risk to go all-in on a memorable Point Of Differentiation.

PRO TIP

Want to out-pace your competition and easily attract more sellers or buyers? Here's the next level of specialization and differentiation for investors: Figure out how you can be #1 in your area for something. It could be the way you do something or who you serve or how you do it. Figure out how to be either the top or the only one.

An example from my own business: there are other copywriters out there who write for many different types of clients including investors, but I'm the only copywriter in the world who writes exclusively for investors.

Maybe you are the only investor in your area who buys house that still have tenants in them; maybe you are the only investor in your area who sells rent-to-own houses that are fully furnished; maybe you are the only investor in your area who speaks Mandarin.

Whatever it is: find it be the only one who does it. And if you get copycats then simply switch your branding to be "the first in the area to…"

CHAPTER 6: YOUR STORY, CHARACTER, AND VOICE

You have figured out who you want to talking to and what makes you different from other real estate investors out there. Now it's time to think about how to communicate with those people. This is how you connect with sellers and buyers.

Your story, character, and voice are critical building blocks of your brand. Most people don't think about them ahead of time but when you do, it makes your marketing more effective…

- You'll be interesting to the right people, capturing their attention by who you are and how you present yourself.
- You'll help your audience know what to expect from you when they interact with you.
- Your marketing will act like a magnet to the people you want to work with and will also filter out the people you don't want to work with.
- You'll create consistency, which helps to make you more credible and trustworthy.

Your story, character, and voice is the "persona" that you approach your marketplace with.

Now, I need to be clear about something; for some investors, creating a story, character, and voice can feel fake. They might wonder: "Why don't you just be yourself?" Some readers might think that pretending to be someone else is a lie. I'm NOT suggesting that you lie. Rather, creating your story, character, and voice is about figuring out the best parts of yourself to present to sellers, and the best parts of yourself to present to buyers, and crafting that to highlight it.

Look, we're all complex people and you can't possibly share ALL of yourself with the people you connect with. Besides, the process of meeting sellers and getting them to sell to you, and the process of meeting buyers and getting them to buy from—those are complex scenarios and you'd never be able to share everything about yourself. So, when you are sharing about yourself in your marketing then it's better to figure out what will resonate with your audience and share that, and skip the parts that will distract them.

One of my clients was struggling to find sellers for his wholesaling business. He had a lot of professional real estate experience and he was trying to present that story in his marketing. However, I realized that his unsophisticated audience wasn't resonating with his professional real estate experience. As I dug deeper, I learned that he had once gone through a foreclosure himself. So we highlighted that in his marketing instead. Rather than coming across as a slick, educated professional with a ton of experience, we pointed out to people going through foreclosure that he knew exactly what they were facing and had discovered a simple solution to their problem.

It wasn't false; we just highlighted a different aspect of his story; one that would much more clearly connect with his motivated seller audience.

And, the very same client started building a list of cash buyers and investor-partners, and to that audience we highlighted a different aspect of his story. Again, we didn't highlight his years of professional real estate experience but rather how he had turned around his financial situation with a few wholesale deals and had gone from foreclosure to financially free through wholesaling.

Same client. Same truths. Just presented differently for different audiences who would be able to appreciate that information from their unique perspective and would relate to it in a way that would help them make a decision about whether it made sense to work with this investor.

There's another reason that you may want to create a story, character, and voice for yourself: do you suffer from fear when you're trying to deal with sellers and buyers? A lot of investors, even the most successful ones, still have a bit of fear when picking up the phone to talk to someone or when going to a seller's house to make an offer.

Creating a story, character, and voice for you is a way to help you deal with that fear in the same way that a superhero sheds his or her "regular person" alibi to become a superhero. Consider the meek and mild-mannered Clark Kent, who leaves his suit and glasses in a phone booth and becomes Superman. In the same way, if you have a story, character, and voice, these act like your superhero cape that you put on when you are in "Investor" mode, and you can more fearlessly approach sellers and buyers... because at the end of the day you go back to your "Normal" mode and the challenges and stresses that you may have faced when talking to sellers and buyers can be left at the office. (This is a secret strategy used by top salespeople who struggle with overcoming rejection in the sales process. When they have character or identity who does the selling, it's that character who experiences the rejection, not the actual person!)

So, let's look at each of these components. These are all inter-related and overlapping so make sure you read through this whole chapter and then work on your story, character, and voice simultaneously.

Your Story

Your story is made up of the key events in your past. To continue the superhero theme for a moment, it's your origin story. Every superhero has an origin story that shows how they became the hero they are today.

When you create a story for yourself, it's an opportunity to build credibility into your background and show your sellers and buyers that you are qualified to help them. (Again, this is a TRUE story; I'm not suggesting you make something up.)

Your story is made up of selected events from your past that are relevant to the audience.

For example, the client I mentioned earlier had a story for sellers—how he was also once in foreclosure. And, he had a story for buyers—how he went from foreclosure to financially free through wholesaling.

Or another example: When I built my Real Estate Investing Copywriter brand, I created a story for myself from the events of my background. I highlight how my dad was a contractor and I would help him when he worked with investors; and later, as an adult, I mention how I was involved in many different kinds of investing transactions and have also wholesaled properties and also currently own rental real estate. That information adds credibility to my brand; it is 100% true but it's a selected list of events that my audience cares about. I've left out that I was a stockbroker for a while and hated it. I've left out that I have an MBA. Those are pieces of my story that I highlight when I work with Wall Street investors or when I've done a bit of business consulting in the past but they're rarely important to real estate investors so I leave it out. I've left out that I was once robbed at gunpoint. I've left out that I once wanted to teach high school English and almost went to college for that. Those are just pieces of the puzzle that make up who I am.

Many investors don't create a story for themselves and therefore miss out on this opportunity to "backdate" credibility into their brand with a story that is true but also interesting. They throw the proverbial baby out with the bathwater—by not talking about themselves at all, they miss out on curating and highlighting the relevant aspects of their background that would resonate with sellers and buyers. Don't skip this opportunity because it's a helpful way to connect with people!

So, what should your story be? Here's how to craft your story…

First, consider who your audiences are. If you work with sellers and with buyers then you may want to have two stories.

Second, think about what is important for those audiences to hear. Some sellers want to relate to the person they are selling their house to; other sellers want to work with an underdog who is "going up against the bureaucratic institutions" like they are; other sellers want someone who is decisive and will just tell them what to do; other sellers want someone who has a more consultive approach.

It will depend on your audience and what kind of motivation they have. Sellers going through foreclosure probably won't want a slick "banker" type of person working with them. Older folks who want to sell so they can extract their equity and retire probably want someone who will guide them through the process with respect and patience. Divorced women probably don't want a macho, in-your-face ex-football player telling them what to do.

Third, think about the events in your life (your whole life, even going back to childhood) that will be relevant.

- If you work with short-on-cash motivated sellers, you might be doing okay now but consider highlighting how your impoverished childhood has given you a desire to help others in the same modest situation.
- If you work with seniors, you might think back to a time when an older relative struggled to afford their retirement because all their equity was locked up in their house.
- If you work with frustrated landlords, consider whether you or a friend or family member ever had the same tenant-related headaches.

Fourth, collect those elements together into a story for each of your audiences. It doesn't need to be complicated or long; just a couple of sentences will do.

Bonus tip: maybe you've had a very fortunate life and haven't had to go through the same struggles that your motivated sellers have faced. Maybe you work with sellers going through foreclosure but there's no foreclosure in your background; maybe you work with seniors who need to sell but you haven't had to watch an elderly relative struggle in their retirement. That's okay. I'd like to share some really practical insight that I learned, of all places, from a psychology professor in college. Someone in class asked this professor about the challenges that counselors face: for example, how could someone provide grief counseling if they've never lost someone close, or how could someone provide marriage counseling if they've never been married. My psych professor wisely pointed out that you may never have lost someone close but you can still relate to people in their grief because you've grieved about *something*; and you may not have been married but you can still provide marriage counseling because you've been in close and trusting relationships. Her point, which I'm stealing and sharing with you, is: you may not have had the *exact* same problem as your motivated seller but you may have had a related problem. You may never have gone through foreclosure but perhaps you've been so short on money that you didn't know if you could pay your bills; you may never had seen an elderly relative struggle to afford retirement but you know what it's like to have family members wonder how much retirement will cost and whether they'll have enough; you may never have gone through divorce but you know what it means to feel betrayed and stuck with pieces of a past relationship that you want to get rid of so you can move on; you may have never faced the complications of inheriting a property but you know the mixed feelings of dealing with the loss of a loved one *and* you know about the challenges of owning a second home.

Therefore, find something relevant in your life that you can connect to your story if you feel like you're at a loss.

Your Character

Your character is who you are today. Often, it's our story that shapes who we are today, which is why I put character second. Your character is your personality, your attitude, your mindset, your domination emotion and thought process; it's often the result of your story.

Your character won't be that much different from who you are right now. It's hard (but not impossible) to have a completely different character than who you are in real life. However, you will still want to think carefully about your character because there's a good chance that you want to highlight only certain aspects of who you are to your audience.

Let me give you an example from my own life. I can be positive and outgoing. I smile a lot. I'm an off-the-scale optimist who loves to laugh. When I get stressed out, I crack jokes (which got me into trouble with the police once… but that's a different story).

But I can also be studious and focused and quiet and contemplative at times. If someone were to confide in me about something, I know enough to turn off the goofiness and listen with empathy.

So, those are the two "sides" of my real-life personality—the highly outgoing side but also a very quiet side. Depending on what is happening when you meet me, your first impression of me might be very different. And, that's the same for everyone.

Now, when I was a stockbroker, a lot of my prospective clients were elderly people who were worried about their pensions and whether their savings would last them through retirement.

Which aspect of my personality do you think I used as my "character" when I was a stockbroker? Yes, I was quiet and respectful and listened with empathy. That doesn't mean I was false to myself, or that I was hiding anything from them, or even that I didn't smile and laugh when appropriate. Rather, it just means that I recognized which aspect of my personality was best suited to the situation.

Natural-born salespeople do this without a second thought but to the rest of the world it can see strange.

So, which aspect of your personality should you highlight as your character when working with your audiences? It probably depends on the audience, right? A family that is struggling financially and facing foreclosure of their family home will appreciate a very different approach than the entrepreneurial-minded cash investor with an "A-type" personality who wants cash flow to replace his income because he'd rather be at the beach than at a job.

Here's how to determine your character…

First, consider who your audiences are. If you work with sellers and with buyers then you may want to have two characters. (Don't worry! It's not hard. If you are being your authentic self yet only highlighting one aspect of your authentic self then it's easy to switch from one to the other. Chances are, you do this already when dealing with some various people throughout your day.)

Second, think about what is important for each of those audiences. Who do they want to deal with? Are they looking for someone who will take charge of a confusing situation? Are they looking for an ally who has empathy? Are they looking for someone who is positive and will assure them that everything is okay? It depends on your audiences.

Third, think about your own personality. Chances are, you are one way among some people and a different way among other people, usually dependent on the situation and the mood. How are you with your friends? How are you with your elderly relatives? How are you with your children? These different relationships will help to reveal the aspect of your character that you can tap into.

Additionally, you may want to think about the emotions that your audiences are feeling when they interact with you (i.e. sellers might feel confusion and fear; buyers might feel hope and optimism) and think about the interactions and relationships in your own life where those feelings have appeared. Here are two examples (but these are, by no means, the only options)…

- If you have a family member facing difficult financial times and they confide in you, how would you interact with them? Use that interaction to inform the kind of character you'll have when interacting with sellers.
- If you have a family member who is flush with cash and wants to find the latest angle, how would you interact with them? Use that interaction to inform the kind of character you'll have when interacting with buyers.

Fourth, jot down some notes about what you are like during those types of interactions.

- What you say
- The tone of your voice
- What your facial expressions are like
- What your body language is like

And, refer to those notes prior to engaging with your audience. Eventually it will become second nature and you won't need your notes but in the early days it will help.

(You'll also find that this is helpful when doing some of your marketing. For example, if you are recording videos for sellers, then use your "seller character" in your video.)

I should point out that some naysayers will read this section above and think that I'm suggesting we create a false persona, which I am absolutely not. Yet to prove what they think, these naysayers will point to ultra-successful people who seem to be authentic and consistent no matter who they talk to. But that's exactly my point: when you craft the right character, you are simply asking yourself, "What qualities and aspects do I already possess that I can highlight for people to help them want to do business with me?" The people who seem to be truly authentic are the ones who have naturally discovered their own character and can switch into that character seamlessly because it is so authentic to who they are.

Your Voice

Now that you have written out your story and character, this part should come very easily because it springs from both. Your voice is the verbal (and written) expression of your story and character. It's your tone and the words you use. In fact, you did a lot of the heavy lifting for this when you were formulating your character just a moment ago.

The reason why you need this last step is because it ensures alignment between your character and what you say to your audience.

Just imagine if you sat down with an elderly grandmother: She is clutching a few papers in her hand and she's confused about what her IRA even is, and whether it will pay for her retirement. Perhaps her spouse recently passed away and she knows she can't afford the house anymore. She is also reluctantly coming around to the fact that she can't make it up the stairs like she used to or keep the house as clean as she would like.

Then you sit down and give her your very best empathetic smile. You reach out and place your hand on hers and nod with confidence. ... *Then you start using highly technical jargon. And you are loud and curse a lot.*

Would any of that have an effect on her? Yeah, it would probably turn her right off. It will force her to retreat into her already scared shell and she'll delay a decision and wait until she feels more comfortable.

That's why you need to think about your voice. All too often we forget who we are dealing with and we use technical jargon that doesn't make sense, or we allow our full personalities to show (instead of our carefully curated characters) and that can turn people off.

So, here is how to make sure your voice is in alignment with your character:

First, consider who your audiences are. If you work with sellers and with buyers then you may need two different voices.

Second, think about what is important for those audiences. Who do they want to hear from you? What words and concepts do they understand? What words and concepts don't they understand? What questions do they have? When do they get confused? When do they completely shut down and stop paying attention. When do they get inspired to take action? Answer as much of this as you can right now. As you interact with them further, refine your answers.

Third, think about your character. What does your character say? How do you say it? What words does your character not say?

Fourth, jot down some notes about what to say when interacting with your audiences.

- Write down specific words.
- Write down specific analogies.
- Write down specific stories and examples.
- Write down specific questions.

Bonus tip: One really simple way to nail down your voice and what to say is to create a flowchart of a typical interaction with a seller or a buyer. Let's say a seller responds to a mailing and calls you and leaves a voicemail. You call them back. List out what the conversation looks like (greeting, introduction, why you are calling, asking why they called, asking about the property, probing for the underlying motivation, looking for a commitment, getting agreement to continue to the next step). That's an example of what your call might be like. Then, considering who your audience is and who your character is, think about what words you want to use.

SHORTCUT

Analogies are powerful tools to use when developing your story, your character, and your voice. An analogy is a comparison between two things, ideally between something unfamiliar and something familiar, in order to clarify the unfamiliar thing. It's also often shorter to say, and it creates a picture in the person's mind.

When telling people about the complicated process of foreclosure, you can call it "complicated"… or you can describe it like being lost in a dark forest with no clear way out. The analogy gives people a real sense of what foreclosure is like and can help them want to take action.

When people ask me what I aspire to in my Real Estate Investing Copywriter business, I tell them that I want to be the Dan Kennedy of real estate investing. That creates a picture right away of how I want my business to run: high-end copywriting and business strategy consultation with a mix of marketing and clear, actionable strategies.

Whenever you are dealing with topics that confuse your audience, the best way to make it clear is to create an analogy.

CHAPTER 7: YOUR BRAND

Think about Apple, McDonald's, and Nike. What do you think about? Chances are, you immediately thought of their very distinctive brands—Apple's apple logo, McDonald's golden arches, and Nike's swoosh.

Of course those symbols aren't the only components that make up those company's brands but they are graphical representations of something much larger. Without realizing it, you thought of even more things than just the apple, the arches, and the swoosh; without realizing it, you thought of the user-friendly trendy popularity of Apple, the salty deliciousness and speedy convenience of McDonald's, and the action-oriented inspiration of Nike. In other words, you didn't just "see" the logo in your mind's eye, you also subconsciously were reminded of the other aspects of the company as well… aspects that each company has carefully cultivated over the years to remind you of whenever you think of them.

A good brand does a lot of work:

- It makes a company memorable
- It filters out the wrong prospects and attracts the right prospects
- It communicates to its prospects about the reasons they should do business with the company
- It reinforces the main marketing messages and the Point Of Differentiation

A good brand is a powerful part of your business!

The Surprising Truth About Brands

When most people are asked what a brand is, their first thought is that it's the logo or the name of the company. While those are two pieces that make up the brand, it's actually so much more.

A brand is the thoughts and feelings you get when you think of that company. A brand is the simple "shorthand" a company has that rapidly communicates its Point Of Differentiation to its target audience. The brand is made up of the company name and logo but also the company's products and services, how it communicates, what it says in the market, and even the reason why people conduct business with that company.

Chances are, you know that already. But here is the surprising truth that most people don't realize: every business has a brand. Yes, every single business. Even your real estate investing company. Even if you've never intentionally thought about a brand before. The only difference is: some people allow their brands to be built by default while others build their brands by design.

Almost worse, some companies create a logo and a catchy name and *think* they've created their brand by design but all they've done is slap a logo and a catchy name on a brand built by default.

Guess which business does better. It shouldn't be any surprise: companies that build their brands by design create far stronger brands (and have far greater success) than companies that allow their brands to be built by default.

Since every business (including your real estate investing business) has a brand, you might as well take charge of your brand and build it intentionally.

Building your brand intentionally gives you the most control over how others see you, whether they do business with you, and what they can expect from you when you work together.

Also, as an investor, you need to make sure you build a brand both for the seller side of your business and for the buyer side. You shouldn't use the same brand for both. (Of course they might have similar elements, if that makes strategic sense, but you're reaching two very different audiences so expect to create two brands).

In fact, you may want even more brands, depending on who your target market is. For example, if you work with motivated sellers who are elderly homeowners that want to extract their equity to pay for their retirement, and if you work with people who are experiencing foreclosure and severe financial distress—those are two *very* different audiences. You might be able to serve them both with brand like "Jim Buys Springfield Houses Fast" but it might make more strategic sense (and be more effective in the long-run) to create two separate brands, one for each.

Brand Building, Simplified

So, how can you create your brand? Well, it starts by knowing your Point Of Differentiation; and then figuring out your story, character, and voice; and then pulling them together into a strategic way that resonates with your audience.

I've been helping real estate investors build brands for years. I've observed, made notes, tested, failed, learned, and succeeded. From all of this work, I've found that there are really just three types of real estate investing brands. (Of course there's a lot of subtle variations within each of these three but these are the three big categories of real estate investing brands, in no particular order.)

The Corporate Brand: With a corporate brand you position the company first. Usually the business name is prominently displayed on the site. There are often images of the properties you work with and images of people on the site are often stock images of ideal customers or professional headshots in an "Our Team" page.

One example of this kind of brand my client Memphis Invest. They have a corporate brand because the name of the company is prominent and the company's communication has more formality to it. Another client's corporate brand is American Wealth Builders.

The corporate brand is the most formal of the three brands. (It doesn't have to be so formal that it seems like you are a robot sent from the future to generate cash flow. After all, real estate investing website creator Investor Carrot is a corporate brand and they are very fun and informal.) That said, it gets its formality from leading with the name of the company rather than the name of a person.

At times, this corporate brand can impart a "big business" feel to your investing company, although that's not always the case, especially if you use the corporate brand approach but work toward a "boutique firm" feel.

This brand scales really well so if your business grows from a one-investor-operation to a team, there is no real impact on the brand itself.

When working with buyers, this brand works well if your clients are experienced investors and high net worth investors.

When working with sellers, some target markets may get a sense of assurance from the structure and professionalism of a corporate-style brand, especially if they are cautious about dealing with individual investors. However, the opposite is true too: if you're trying to attract motivated sellers in financial distress, they may prefer to work with a company that doesn't seem like it's a corporation because they are likely frustrated by the bureaucracy of organizations.

I should warn you, though, that there are so many corporate brands out there already (most done poorly), and many of them go by names like: "St. Louis Homebuyers" or "Phoenix Financial Freedom Corp" so you need to find a way to be unique among them.

The Celebrity Brand (or) The Lifestyle Brand: The celebrity brand positions YOU as the brand. You're the rockstar investing expert who can help sellers sell fast or buyers buy for massive cash flow. Sometimes it's all about you and your larger-than-life personality but sometimes it's about your lifestyle and how real estate investing lets you live your life on your terms.

Before he became President, Donald Trump (not a client) was a real estate investor and he's an excellent example of a celebrity brand: he's got a massive personality that is notable and magnetizes people, and his gold-plated lifestyle also adds to the brand.

One of my clients, Mark Evans "The DM", loves to travel the world so we have positioned him as a world-traveling virtual investor (meaning he can invest no matter where he happens to be).

Another client, Sunil Tulsiani of the Private Investment Club, has positioned himself as "The Wealthy Cop" because he used to be a police officer and is now a full-time investor and founder of an investment club.

The celebrity brand is usually far less formal than the corporate brand. The person themselves (or the lifestyle they live) is front and center. Sure, the buyer might write checks to the celebrity's legal entity but the *brand* is driven by the person themselves.

All the content in this brand—from websites to blogs to emails to images—all center around the person or their lifestyle. In some cases (with a few exceptions) a lot of the content will come from you, so your blog might say things like: "I was climbing in the Himalayas last week when an investor called to do a deal." The language is "I", "Me", "My" to help establish YOU as the brand.

This brand is harder to scale because the entire brand is built around one person and that can sometimes cause confusion among investors if they think the one investor is doing everything behind the scenes. (There are ways around this, such as by mentioning that you have a team). It's not impossible to scale but there can be challenges.

This brand is also harder to break free from if you want to do something else or if you start on the wrong foot. One example (outside of the real estate investing space) is Tim Ferriss and his Four Hour Work Week. This is a celebrity/lifestyle brand that all started with his book *The Four Hour Work Week*. Tim has said publicly that the "four hour" component of his brand has been both a blessing and a curse: A blessing because it's so memorable but a curse because everyone thinks that Tim really only works four hours a week when even he admits that it's not true.

This brand works well if you have a great angle and/or a big personality or ego. (Nothing wrong with that). For an angle, you need something that will attract your ideal target market. For example, investing from the beach, or cellphone investing, or investing in your underwear, or investing by the pool, or investing from your South American villa, or investing from your private jet, or investing from your motorcycle, etc. See where I'm going with this? Your angle needs to be some attractive aspect of your lifestyle that makes other investors think: "I want that!"

When working with buyers, this brand works well to attract new or experienced investors (and depending on your brand, you can increase one or the other).

When working with sellers, you can still use this brand but you have to take it in a totally different direction since you don't want to put a *flashy* lifestyle as the front-and-center piece when you're talking to motivated sellers. However, there are plenty of "Jim Buys Ugly Houses" brands that have the makings of being a celebrity brand but are never really taken far enough by the company. When done well, this can be very effective.

Note: if you don't like the spotlight, don't pick this brand. However, this is probably the fastest way to create a unique brand if you are still looking for a Point Of Differentiation.

The Educational Brand: The educational brand is, as the name suggests, focused on educating others. The entire brand is built around showing others how to achieve their goal, whatever that goal might be (selling fast, buying for cash flow, flipping, wholesaling, whatever).

This type of brand is slightly more formal (like the corporate brand) but most importantly has a layer of instruction to it.

This is a great brand to build if you want to attract brand new investors or if you want to focus on building a passive income stream of information and coaching. My client REIN (the Real Estate Investment Network, a Canadian network of investors) does this very effectively. Another investor who does this well is the one and only Rich Dad, Robert Kiyosaki. Need I also mention BiggerPockets? Or "the guys" of The Real Estate Guys Radio Show? These brands are all about education (while the people who run them may choose to leverage their students to sell properties, information, or other services to).

The potential is also here to attract sellers by educating them, however I've seen a lot of seller education brands struggle for two reasons: first, because they potentially educate sellers out of selling; and second, because education can be a long-term play (with your profit coming from a future purchase) but working with sellers is often a one-time transaction. I'm not saying it's impossible to build a seller education brand; I'm just pointing out the challenge.

When done appropriately, you can do deals with your students using an educational brand, you just need to be cautious that you don't come out of the gate swinging with deals when the student might want to take a slower approach. One challenge, however, is that many people start out as real estate investing students and they *stay* as students and rarely move forward. So, a component of your education should include encouraging them or enticing them to take action.

In many ways, this brand straddles the fence between the formality of the corporate brand (which tends to be more trusted among students) and the lifestyle aspect of the celebrity lifestyle brand (which tends to attract more students), but the most important thing is to give good instruction. The more instruction you give (the more step-by-step and easy-to-follow instruction!) the better your students will be at becoming your investing clients.

This brand can be easier to scale because a lot of the information can be automated through autoresponders and video and PDF ebooks/reports, so it can take a lot of work to set up initially but you can potentially do a lot of deals to your students later.

There are many educational brands out there (and it's growing all the time) so you need to find your own unique angle.

So What Should You Do?

If you're not sure where to start, consider the following:

Consider who your ideal target market is. The more experienced your buyers are, the more formal they may want to be. (i.e. they may not necessarily be attracted to education or your lifestyle). I have a client who is somewhat famous before becoming an investor and we were going to build a celebrity brand for him... until we analyzed his target market and realized that they were actually more famous than he was. So it wouldn't make sense to go with a celebrity brand, instead we're building a corporate brand.

Think about whether you want to build multiple brands (one for sellers and one for buyers, which you should do if you are using a celebrity model for buyers -- you need something for sellers) or whether you only want to build one brand (which is easier to do when using the corporate brand). With a corporate brand, you can put a buyers side and a sellers side on the same website pretty easily. With a celebrity brand, you should only focus on one and keep the other very separate. In addition, remember this: you don't have to have the same type of brand for buyers and sellers. You may choose to create an educational brand for your buyer market and a corporate brand for your seller market.

Decide if you like the spotlight or not. (Nothing wrong if you do; nothing wrong if you don't... either way, it helps to inform you of the direction to take).

Narrow your focus a little and then test out each approach. You don't have to invest a lot of time or money but just do a bit of brainstorming and think about whether you can sustain a one-post-a-week celebrity lifestyle blog for a year, or whether you have the experience to deliver helpful education to students.

Now It's Time To Build Your Brand

Here's the good news: you don't need an MBA to build a simple brand; you just need to have done the work that I've outlined in this book.

1. Think about who your target market is and what would resonate with them. (Remember: you'll probably want to build at least one brand for sellers and one brand for buyers.)
2. Think about the WIIFM+ROI combination and what your audience needs to hear to take action.
3. Think about who your competition is and how you can out-compete them.
4. Think about what your Point Of Differentiation is, and how to incorporate that into your brand.
5. Think about your story, character, and voice, and how those pieces will be communicated.
6. Gather those together and simplify them into the style of your chosen brand (corporate, celebrity/lifestyle, or educational).
7. Try to come up with a few short and compelling words that summarize all these pieces while also keeping it clear to your audience what you do. This will likely become the name of your company (or perhaps influence your company's slogan or tagline).
8. Keep reading this book all the way through because there may be some other pieces that will prompt you to come back to this chapter and make adjustments to your brand.
9. Solidify your name and ask a few people what they think of it.
10. Hire a designer to create a logo around that name. There are many great designers but I've got a great connection for you in my secret bonus page: RealEstateInvestingCopywriter.com/bonus/playbookbonus.

That's it. A brand is really simple to create and when it clicks for you, you can build a strong and memorable business around it.

PART 3: YOUR BUSINESS

A key part of your marketing and copywriting is understanding your business. Now, you might be thinking: "But I already understand my business." However, as you dig into the chapters in this Part of the book, you'll see that you are going deeper than you ever have before.

There's a very good reason for it: in this Part of the book you will be building a strong foundation that will clearly show you exactly what marketing you need to do, when, and to whom.

By the end of Part 3, you'll have drawn out the sales funnel of your business and that will serve you for the rest of your life as one of the most valuable tools in your business to generate more leads, convert more of them into deals, and make more money from every deal.

CHAPTER 8: YOUR BUSINESS MODEL

"I'm sending out direct mail but it's just not working… what should I change?" the investor asked me.

I paused for a moment. Then gave this answer…

"Before I can answer that question, I need to ask you a question: what's your business model?"

I'm frequently asked the first question by investors, and I frequently ask the second question of investors before I give an answer.

That's because your business model can instantly tell me a lot about your business. The answer to this question helps me to figure out the fastest way to help someone, since some of my ideas and recommendations might apply to one business model but not another.

A business model is "business speak" for the type of business that you own; it reveals how you find clients (in this case: sellers and buyers), how you advertise, and how you make money… all summarized in just a few words.

If you tell someone what your business model is, they can usually get a fairly quick idea of what you do. Most businesses fall into certain patterns that can be described in just a couple of words: wholesaling is a business model. Flipping is a business model. Selling real estate notes is a business model. Owning a fast food restaurant is a business model.

By mentioning one of those, you quickly get a fairly clear idea what they do—what they sell, who they sell to, and how they make money.

Of course it won't tell you *everything* but it's a starting point. It's a piece of information that instantly clarifies and filters.

When an investor tells me that their direct mail isn't working for them, and I ask what their business model is, then I know that, in general a wholesaler is probably using direct mail to find motivated sellers but a rehabber might be using direct mail to find motivated sellers OR retail buyers, while a new developer might be looking for retail buyers.

Of course there might be variations on those business models. For example, you might be a "pure" wholesaler who just puts properties under contract and then wholesales those properties as-is to cash buyers, or you might be a *turnkey* wholesaler who acquires properties and adds value by cleaning them up and adding a tenant and property management before wholesaling them to cash buyers.

And here's an interesting fact about real estate investors: unlike other businesses, many real estate investors have a unique business model in that they need to "sell" to acquire their inventory and to sell it!

(What I mean is: a grocery store didn't have to put up bandit signs to try and find a supplier to supply them with groceries! But we real estate investors need to market to find our "inventory" and then negotiate and "sell" to the seller why we should by from them at a discount!)

Why Does Your Business Model Matter?

Knowing your business model tells you what kinds of relationships you need to have. For example: a wholesaler might need to work with a lot of birddogs, whereas a rehabber may need to build relationships with contractors, while a buy-and-hold rental owner needs to build a strong relationship with a property management company.

Knowing your business model also helps you to know what equipment and infrastructure you need in your business. A wholesaler who takes calls from motivated sellers obviously needs a phone or Skype (or a virtual assistant with the ability to take calls). A wholesaler might have a very different Customer Relationship Management (CRM) system in their business than a rehabber. A rehabber who does it all themselves probably needs access to a truck, whereas a rehabber who owns a big rehabbing empire probably has no use for a truck because everything is delegated to a team.

Knowing your business model also helps you to know what kind of marketing activities you need to do. As a wholesaler, for example, you'll know that you need to market to find motivated sellers and maybe cash buyers, but you market to those groups very differently. As a rehabber wit amazing relationships with real estate agents, maybe you just need marketing to find retail buyers because your acquisitions are already sourced without any marketing needed.

Knowing your business model helps you to know where in your business the revenue-generating parts are (and how to create more value for your buyers and profit for yourself). Understanding your business model will help you get some ranges of numbers to work with when it comes to costs, revenue, profit, and more.

Knowing your business model helps you spot opportunities to grow by expanding different aspects of your business. For example, one very common way to grow is for turnkey wholesalers (who are building a list of cash buyers) to become a "guru" and teach others how to become wholesalers… since many of those students may become cash buyers themselves when they realize that there can be a lot of work in turnkey wholesaling but what they really want to do is enjoy the passive cash flow of owning rental property.

Types Of Business Models

Let's look at the different types of business models. And just a couple of quick point of clarification: (1) we're talking about a typical approach here. There will be variations and some investors will refine their approach very specifically. (2) I haven't provided a comprehensive list below; just a few of the common ones. (3) It is very common to be more than one of these.

- **New developer**: Acquires land and builds on it.
- **Wholesaler**: Acquires a below-market property and then wholesales the contract to a buyer.
- **Turnkey wholesaler**: Acquires a below-market property, adds value by cleaning/fixing the property, placing a tenant, and putting a management company in place, and then sells the property to a buyer.
- **Rehabber**: Acquires a property, fixes it up, and sells the property.
- **Buy-and-hold cash flow investor**: Acquires a property and rents that property to a tenant, then enjoys the cash flow.
- **Expert/Guru**: Teaches other people some aspect of real estate investing.

Of course there are many others, plus complex variations of these (such as a rehabber of single family residences, a rehabber of multi-family residences, a rehabber of manufactured homes, a rehabber of commercial properties, etc.) but this is a start. Do you know what your business model is?

What To Do With This Information

Most newbie investors don't think through this information before proclaiming "I want to be a real estate investor!" Then they try to figure out what that means.

Eventually they discover what you probably already know (even if you've never used the term "business model" before)... investors discover that there are multiple business models in the real estate investing world, and each one is really a different way to make money in investing.

Identifying what your business model is (again, even if you've never used the term before, you've still probably identified your business model!) is the first step in knowing a lot about your business and you will use this information in the very next chapter about sales funnels… because your business model tells you how many sales funnels you need and what those sales funnels need to do.

Knowing your business model also allows you to identify contingencies. If you're a rehabber who typically sells to retail buyers, but your market has become really slow lately for that kind of sale, maybe you start to explore other business models as a contingency—consider becoming a buy-and-hold investor, for example, and branch into another business model to make sure that you keep your deals moving.

There's another reason that you probably want to think about your business model: because investors often are opportunists and it's easy for many investors to jump from one type of investing to another. They're wholesalers one day and then they're rehabbers another day. To those investors, they're just doing different aspects of investing but my recommendation is: pick on business model and work on it until it is working for you. Figure it out and get it dialed in before you jump to another business model. Skipping around from one type of investing to another is a surefire way to spend a lot of money and struggle at all of them. So, pick your business model and focus.

Which leads me to another reason why you want to know your business model: as you grow, you'll want to seek out mentors, coaches, and consultants who can help you. It's useful if you seek out those who have figured out the same business model that you're trying to figure out. Then you'll know exactly who to follow, and also whose insight might not be as valuable to you.

And finally, knowing your business model lets you figure out how you can grow your business. Maybe you're rehabbing single family residences right now. Does it make sense to become a wholesaler? Well, it might it your marketing is bringing you more deals than you can rehab. Or, maybe for a different rehabber, it makes more sense to grow from single family residences to multi-family. Knowing your business model lets you understand which low-hanging fruit are the best choices to grow your business in new ways without having to start from scratch each time.

CHAPTER 9: YOUR SALES FUNNEL

Perhaps you've heard of a sales funnel. The concept has been around for a long time, although more and more people are only starting to become aware of them now. Think of a sales funnel as the path that someone follows to make a commitment to a business—they start out unaware of your business but after you market to them and build a relationship with them and then sell to them, they become a client.

Just a quick disclaimer: This is the longest chapter in the book and it's highly strategic but also highly actionable. I'm passionate about this topic (my MBA dissertation was about sales funnel analysis, and my first book, *The Sales Funnel Bible* was about sales funnels for businesses). I dig into sales funnels in a big way in this chapter because I love the topic but more importantly because I think sales funnels are the biggest opportunity for real estate investors to grow their businesses, yet I'm shocked at how few investors know what a funnel even is (and many haven't heard of it before). As a copywriter for real estate investors, my work always starts with in-depth strategy of an investor's funnel so I can be sure that my copy is as effective as it can be. The more time we spend on your funnel, the better your business will be in every other aspect.

So, let's dig into sales funnels and discover this huge opportunity for you…

A Sales Funnel—What It Is And Why It Should Be Important To You

Imagine that you want to buy a new computer. Perhaps you find a flyer or you see a commercial on TV about some great prices on a computer at a nearby computer store. So you go to the store, talk to a salesperson, and they show you a computer that you like. You buy it. You've just been through that store's sales funnel: You started with a need at the very "top" of their funnel, and you probably didn't even think of the store at first! Then you progressed through a series of interactions with the store (through their advertising and then when you went into the store) and finally you made a commitment to the store by buying the computer.

It doesn't matter what a business sells, all sales funnels follow this basic path: Someone has a problem, then they become aware of what you're selling (and realize that it might solve their problem), then they indicate that they might be interested in learning more, then they show real interest in what you have to sell, then they buy from you.

The sales funnel usually starts at a point where the person has never heard of you before. Then, through various marketing and relationship-building processes, they hear from you and get to know you. And, as their interest grows in what you have to offer, they seek to learn more and more. As their interest increases and as they learn, they progress down the path and, ideally, they say "yes" to make a commitment.

With some variations, that's the basic sales funnel. That sales funnel could be really fast (someone could go through a funnel very quickly if they are looking for some chewing gum), or it could be really slow (someone could take month to go through a funnel if they are looking to buy a house). It's the same *very basic* steps but different speeds.

Frequently, the words used in many businesses are "Lead", "Prospect", and "Customer" but the exact titles differ in each type of transaction, and they definitely differ for real estate investors. But the exact terminology doesn't really matter—real estate investing sales funnels are fundamentally the path that someone follows to make a commitment.

This is true whether we're talking about a wholesaler or a landlord or a flipper or an investing expert who sells coaching to other investors. In all of these cases, at the most fundamental level, the sales funnel describes the path that someone takes toward a commitment.

Why should you pay attention to your sales funnel? Here are just a few reasons:

1. Understanding your sales funnel gives you the steps that you currently take to do deals, and shows you were you can add new ideas and pursue new opportunities to do more deals.
2. Your sales funnel gives you the basic outline of your interaction with sellers, buyers, or whoever you do deals with, and allows you to add data at each part of the interaction. The data can tell you a lot about the success or struggle of your business.
3. Your sales funnel can also help you see where things are broken. For example, if lots of sellers call you in response to your postcard but you don't do deals with very many of them, then you can zoom in on the point right after those calls and test different ways to keep more of those sellers moving through.
4. Your sales funnel is the simplest place to start when you want to make more money, keep more of that money as profit, and scale your business larger.
5. Every business (including every investing business) already has a sales funnel, whether or not you were intentional in building it. So why no intentionally build it?

A sales funnel is a simple yet robust tool that every investor should have built for their business.

Sales Funnels 101

You've just learned the high level basics of what sales funnels are and why they are important. Now let's dig into the pieces that make up your sales funnel.

Again, our starting point is the idea that sales funnels are the path that someone would take to make a commitment to your business.

That "someone" could be any of the following, depending on the kind of investing business you have. (And you may have more than one funnel in your investing business if you work with sellers and with buyers, for example):

- A motivated seller
- A cash buyer
- A JV partner
- A tenant
- A retailer buyer
- An investor who wants to learn about investing
- Anyone who you do business with

Those are the people going through the funnels. And, the commitment they're making could be anything that your investing business does:

- A motivated seller putting their home under contract
- An investor-buyer buying a wholesale contract from you
- A tenant agreeing to rent for a year and handing over the first month's rent
- A retail buyer paying their deposit
- An investor who clicks the "buy now" button for your coaching
- Anyone who you do business with who says "yes" because they want whatever you're offering

It doesn't matter what kind of real estate investing business you're in, it doesn't matter what local market you invest in, it doesn't matter whether you deal with individual sellers or corporations, if you get people to make a commitment then you run them through a path toward that commitment…

… and that path is your sales funnel.

This sales funnel is the path people take to make a commitment to you, and fundamentally the concept is same no matter what kind of real estate investing you do. But, the sales funnel looks different for every business model and for investor—from the labels you use to the activities you do to the number of steps it takes to get to the commitment. Every investor has a sales funnel that drives people toward a commitment but that sales funnel will look different.

In general, here are the big pieces that will be common to every investing funnel. Starting from the big group at the top, and descending into your funnel:

1. Target market
2. Leads
3. Prospects
4. Clients

Target market: In general, your Target Market is the great big group of people who you are trying to connect with. They likely won't have heard of you. They usually have some shared qualities that help you identify who they are. For example, maybe your target market of sellers are absentee owners who own bungalows in Minneapolis. Or maybe your target market of buyers are sophisticated investors who purchase apartments of 10 units or more. Your Target Market is the big group of people at the top of your sales funnel – the group that you are trying to reach.

Leads. Once you connect with this target market and attract them, they become Leads, usually through some indication that they are within your target market and potentially interested in what you have to offer. (Leads may self-indicate that they are leads, as is the case of someone who subscribes to an email list; however, this is not always the case. You might end up with a list of absentee owners that you send postcards to. These are your leads and they are not necessarily self-appointed).

Prospects. As you work with these leads, some will rise to the top as being ideally motivated and suitable to move forward. These people become Prospects as they share additional information about their situation and about how you can help them. Although leads do not always self-indicate their interest, by the time someone becomes a prospect it should be clear that they have some interest in what you have to offer. They might not end up doing a deal but they could.

Clients. This label is a little more complicated! Most sales funnels will call this label "Clients" but investors tend to refer to their clients as "sellers" or "cash buyers" (or other labels). From among these prospects you close the deal and a few become Clients—people who actually complete a transaction with you. Perhaps they sign a contract or they hand over a deposit, so these might be motivated sellers in a seller sales funnel or it might be an investor-buyer in a buyer sales funnel. The key concept here is a commitment—these people make some kind of official, definite acceptance of what you offer. Of all of the terms listed, "Client" tends to throw investors off the most because it's usually a term associated with a retail buyer. Don't get hung up on the use of the word "Client". The point here is that the person (whether they're a seller or buyer or anyone else) is making a commitment to you.

These are the basic terms and concepts you need to know and whenever you read about sales funnels in other books or websites, these terms are common and will translate to your funnel.

If you are brand new to sales funnels or investing then I want to use a non-investing example to illustrate these concepts so you can see how they work in your life. Then it will be easier to build the connection on real estate investing funnels once you go through a funnel that might be more familiar to you: We've probably all purchased a car before so let's imagine a car dealership's sales funnel, to use that as an example.

The car dealership has a Target Market, and it's likely made up of people who have a driver's license, who can afford a car (either with cash or, more likely, because their credit is good enough to get a loan), and people who live in a certain geographic area (so they can get to the dealership to see the car).

The car dealership advertises a huge promotion in a flyer to the neighborhood its Target Market lives in. Some people come into the dealership and express interest in learning more or they go to the dealership's website and sign up with their email to get notified about upcoming special deals. These people have become Leads.

The dealership then works with the Leads to build a relationship, to increase interest, and to make sure that the Leads qualify (i.e. they have a driver's license and can afford to purchase the car). Those that qualify then become Prospects. Prospects are shown several different cars, encouraged to take a test drive, and then asked if they'd like to buy.

Those that buy become Clients. They pay a deposit, have their credit checked, and drive away with a shiny new car.

This is a typical car dealership sales funnel. It can take place over a single day (the flyer shows up in the mailbox in the morning and by the evening person has bought a car). Or, it can take the place over several months (perhaps the person is taking a while to shop for a car and wants to test drive a bunch of different models at different dealerships). And even though I described it as a "typical" sales funnel, there are many variations from one dealership to the next, and depending on other factors such as if the dealership has different brands for different target markets, and so on.

Every business has a sales funnel. It will look different than the one I outlined for the car dealership but the fundamentals are the same. It doesn't matter if a business sells cars (as in the example above), burgers, military jets, lumber, discount merchandise, consulting services, dental services, real estate, or anything else. Every business in the world operates with a sales funnel of some kind even if they don't realize they do. That's why I'm so adamant about understanding and building your sales funnel intentionally – because your real estate investing business already has a sales funnel so you should grow it and leverage it for greater success in your business.

So far, I've laid the groundwork of what sales funnels are and why you need to know them. Now let's talk about how to build one for your business.

Your real estate investing business has a sales funnel. (Actually, it has more than one—perhaps one for sellers, one for buyers, one for tenants, maybe even one so you can attract bird dogs). So it only makes sense that you work on developing your sales funnel to grow your investing business. The more you master your sales funnel and grow it, the more successful you'll become. In all the years I've worked with real estate investors, those who have mastered and grown their sales funnels are the ONLY ones to have succeeded.

So let's start by talking about sales funnel basics and how they work in real estate investing:

Real Estate Investing Sales Funnels

I've shared the basics of funnels with you above. I tried to connect it to some funnels in non-investing businesses to give you a foundation of what funnels are and how they work. Now let's look at funnels that are specific to real estate investors.

Most non-investing businesses have one funnel—to get one group of people through the door or to their website. But real estate investors? We're a different breed and our business requires multiple funnels—for sellers, buyers, tenants, and coaching students… and even more specific than that if you are marketing in one way for motivated sellers and a different way for burnt out landlords… and even more varied than that if you are also doing wholesale deals and rehab deals.

One of my clients, Joe, runs an 8-figure investing empire that includes turnkey wholesaling, rehabbing, new development, buy-and-holds, a coaching mastermind, a real estate brokerage, multiple books and speaking, and a couple other businesses (and a charitable organization) too. He has more sales funnels than just about any other investor I've ever met, but he's mastered them and outsourced them, which gives him a ton of free time to grow his business and enjoy the rewards of his success. Of course you don't have to have that many sales funnels in your business—many investors just start with one or two funnels—but I wanted to share an example of someone who has it really dialed in.

Seller funnel: Here is a common sales funnel that real estate investors use to get sellers:

1. The investor identifies a Target Market of absentee owners within a specific geographic area.
2. The investor rents a list of absentee owners, and that list is the investor's Leads.
3. The investor sends out "I'll buy your home for cash" postcards to that group, and people respond with interest. They become Prospects at this point. The investor works with these Prospects to help them understand the process and to nurture a relationship with them. Not all people who responded to the postcard will be right to do a deal with, so the investor also needs to qualify these Prospects.
4. The investor works with this list of Prospects and makes them an offer on their house. A few will sign the contract, thereby making a commitment and becoming a Client.

It's a very simple model and different pieces of it can be swapped out to work with a different group of people. For example, an investor can build a nearly-identical seller funnel but with different leads—maybe of people who inherited a property, or people in financial distress, or people going through divorce (just to name a few). The sales funnel is basically the same but a few pieces inside the funnel might be different: the direct mail might change, the methods used to build a relationship with the seller might change, the contracts that the seller signs might change.

Meanwhile, the real estate investor also needs buyers so they have a different funnel set up to find cash buyers:

Buyer funnel: Here is a common funnel that real estate investors use to get buyers:

1. The investor identifies a Target Market of people who are not happy with their stock market returns and want to start generating passive cash flow.

2. The investor sets up a website to capture email, then uses social media to send people to that website. The people who share their contact information become Leads.
3. The investor builds a relationship with these Leads and asks them what they're looking for. The Leads reply to the emails, they interact with the investor on social media, and it becomes apparent which investors are ready to invest sooner and have the capital to do so. These people become Prospects.
4. Then, the investor finds a deal and emails it to the list of Prospects. One of those prospects becomes agrees to do the deal and sends their money to the investor, thereby becoming a Client.

This too is a very simple model, and different pieces of it can be swapped out to work with a different group of people: for example, an investor can build a nearly-identical buyer funnel but with different leads—maybe of people at their local real estate investing association (REIA) instead of from social media.

And, these are just two examples—an example of a seller sales funnel and an example of a buyer sales funnel. And even within these basic funnel frameworks, every investor is going to have a slightly different funnel depending on many factors, such as:

- How many seller and buyer target markets they work with
- Where they find those people (i.e. a list to rent, or from social media, or some other source)
- What kind of real estate they work with (residential, commercial, undeveloped land)
- What kind of deals they do (buy and hold, flip, rental, wholesale)
- Whether they do the work themselves or use a team
- And many other factors

You can take two investors using the same basic seller funnel or buyer funnel, and they could each create what seems to be an entirely different, unique funnel. It will probably follow the basic format I've listed above but the tactics will all be different.

How To Build Your Real Estate Investing Sales Funnel

Here's a step by step way to build your sales funnel:

Step 1. Identify your basic business model. First, if you're brand new to real estate investing, you'll need to figure out what kind of investing you're going to do. Are you a rehabber? A cash flow investor? Wholesaler? Each of those types of investing will require their own sales funnel. You can't create one funnel for all of them. If you try to squeeze all of your investing efforts into one sales funnel, it will become muddled and anyone you put into your sales funnel will not work their way toward doing a deal with you.

It's okay if you don't know exactly what kind of investor you want to be; it's okay if you change your mind later; it's okay if you want to do several things. But for now you'll need to choose one sales funnel to build. (You can always tweak it after if needed).

Step 2. Decide how many sales funnels you need. Chances are, you'll probably need a seller sales funnel so you can find deals, and some kind of buyer or tenant sales funnel so you can exit those deals if you're not a buy-and-hold investor. You might need more sales funnels but there's a good chance you'll need at least the two I've mentioned here. I'm a real estate investor too and I have a couple of different buyer and seller sales funnels including: a buyer sales funnel for American investors who are looking for turnkey rental properties, and another one for Canadian investors who are looking for undeveloped land. Those are two very different groups and so I've set up a separate funnel for each one.

Step 3. Build your basic funnel. Next you need to lay out the high level view of your funnel. Just the big picture—usually about 4-5 steps or so, similar to what I did for you earlier in the chapter. You don't need to know the exact tactics, just start with the high level. This is like framing in a house. You can't actually live comfortably in the house just yet but you know where the walls are.

Here's a chart to show how it works. First, draw a chart like this:

#	Step	Details
1	Target market	
2	Leads	
3	Prospects	
4	Clients	

Then, fill out the chart with your details:

#	Step	Details
1	Target market	Absentee owners.
2	Leads	Rent a list of absentee owners. Postcard is mailed to this group.
3	Prospects	People respond to the postcard by phone. I arrange a meeting and educate them on how it works. Then I make an offer on their house.
4	Clients	They accept my offer and we sign the contract.

See? It's just really simple.

Step 4. Add specific strategies and steps to your funnel. Now it's just a matter of filling things in step-by-step. These pieces may need to be adjusted over time, perhaps because you discover it doesn't work the way you thought or because of competition or the market shifts or you tested something and learn a better approach.

The goal here is to create a simple one-sheet that outlines your whole business at a glance and you can follow these steps (or hand some or all of the pieces off to someone else). So, you might add to your chart like this:

#	Step	Details
1	Target market	Absentee owners. 1. Refer to Avatar profile. 2. Identify zip codes to target.
2	Leads	Rent a list of absentee owners. Postcard is mailed to this group. 3. Sign in to ABC List Rental Company and find the absentee owner list for preferred zip code. 4. Pay for the list. 5. Download the list. 6. Sign in to XYZ Postcard Company. 7. Upload the list of leads. 8. Select postcard template #4. 9. Pay to mail to the list of leads.

#	Step	Details
3	Prospects	People respond to the postcard by phone. I arrange a meeting and educate them on how it works. Then I make an offer on their house. 10. Double check my answering machine message. 11. Make sure I have my checklist by the phone. 12. Answer calls as they come in. (Or call back those who left a message.) 13. Run through checklist with each caller. 14. Enter information into my Prospect Spreadsheet as they answer the points on the checklist. 15. Schedule an appointment. 16. Attend the appointment. 17. Hand them my information. 18. Go through the information. 19. Handle objections. 20. Ask for the deal.
4	Clients	They accept my offer and we sign the contract. 21. Sign the contract. 22. Pay them a deposit. 23. Send information to title company. 24. Attend meeting at title company to finalize purchase.

Of course the information may be different for you, and you may want to make it even more detailed, but this shows you how to build your funnel very simply, step-by-step.

As your business grows, your funnel will become more complex. Here are the first couple of steps of a buyer funnel to show you how to deal with the complexity.

#	Step	Details
1	Target market	People who are not happy with stock market returns. 1. Refer to Avatar profile. 2. Make sure a landing page with email

		capture is set up.
2	Leads	Connect with people in various settings and talk about how you can get better returns in real estate. 3. Post on Facebook, LinkedIn, YouTube, and Instagram daily. Talk about the economy, the stock market, and real estate returns. 4. Link to the landing page in every post. 5. Reply to all comments and direct messages in these sites, inviting people to go to the landing page. 6. Run Facebook ads targeting people who fit the Avatar profile sending them to the landing page.

(and so on).

So, you've built the basic chart, then "framed in" your funnel with some specifics, then added details. Don't think of this as a "once-and-done" effort. This is something you build and adjust all the time. It's a working document that you will use in your business forever.

Step 5. Deploy. This is what I love about sales funnels. They just lay out step-by-step what you need to build and then run to do deals in your business. If there are accounts that need to be set up or websites that need to be built, this is where you set-up and build those things. Ultimately, you want to create everything now, as quickly as you can, so that you can start doing deals.

(Note: While deploying, you may find that you need to adjust certain things in your funnel. That's okay! This chart will help you stay on track to keep building.)

Step 6. Run, Test, Revise. Once you've built your funnel(s), then you can start running them by just going through each step and doing what the step calls for. Try to run a few deals through your funnel and be prepared to adjust your funnel. You might find, for example, that you miss too many calls from people replying to your postcards. That's not a failure, it's a sales funnel data point, which allows you to adjust your sales funnel to get it working again. For example, to solve the missed call problem, send everyone to a voicemail and call them back at your convenience.

By taking this approach, you'll instantly see where things are breaking in your sales funnel and you can fix them quickly and clearly (without making the common mistake of assuming that your whole business is broken when instead it's just one small step in your funnel).

While you run deals through your funnel, collect data on these deals. For example, create a spreadsheet and put your sales funnel steps into the spreadsheet, and then add data as you get it—how many postcards you send out, how many people call back, how many people agree to a meeting, how many contracts you close. These numbers give you specific ratios that allow you to measure how your sales funnel is doing. Then, when you make adjustments to your funnel, you can see what the actual impact is to your numbers. For example, if you change your postcards and see a big drop in the number of people who call you, then you know that the postcard might not work the way you want so you can go back to the old postcard and try something different.

Summary

Every business (including every real estate investing business) has one or more sales funnels. However, not all businesses intentionally work on their funnels. When you intentionally work on yours, you'll open up a world of opportunity and growth, building a business that is based on data instead of guesswork, and allowing you to scale your business like never before.

BONUS: Your sales funnel is one of the most important parts of your marketing strategy. So, I've created several additional sales funnel resources for you here:
RealEstateInvestingCopywriter.com/bonus/playbookbonus

CHAPTER 10: YOUR MARKETING

Your business model will tell you what your sales funnel(s) should be like. Your sales funnel(s) will tell you what your marketing should be like. The three work together but you have to do them in order.

How Your Business Model And Sales Funnel Guide Your Marketing

Your business model and sales funnel will show you exactly what you need to do. In fact, while designing your sales funnel, you probably already started to see where the pieces of your marketing started to fit together.

For example, for motivated sellers, perhaps you saw that the rented mailing list would give you addresses for your direct mail, which you will send out, then prospective sellers will respond to by calling the number on the direct mail, then you'll connect with those people and make offers, then you'll go to their house and close them. (That's just one seller example. Of course it will be slightly different for everyone, depending on your business model and sales funnel.)

So, each of those steps in your sales funnel become a "touchpoint" where you need to figure out what kind of marketing you need there.

In the example above, you'll need the following marketing content:

1. You're sending out some kind of direct mail, so you'll need **direct mail** as one marketing piece.
2. Then they're calling you back so you'll need someone to answer the phone (you or a virtual assistant) or a voicemail, which means you'll need **phone scripts** for you or your VA, or for your voicemail and for whomever calls the seller back.
3. And when you go to their home to view the house and make an offer, you'll probably need some **educational material** that you can use to walk them through the offer.

So, there are your basic pieces for that particular business model and sales funnel. Over time, you might add more—perhaps you'll test Yellow Letters versus postcards; perhaps you'll do bandit signs; perhaps you'll want some credibility pieces on a website to help people make a decision.

But it all starts with your business model and sales funnel. Figure out what those are and your marketing steps will reveal themselves. Then you can build from there.

You Have One Goal

If marketing seems weird, mysterious, or complicated to you, let me simplify it for you: You have just ONE single goal with your marketing... ***you need to nurture more of the right people through your funnel.***

Yeah, that's a lot of "marketing lingo" but when you understand what it means, it helps to clarify what you need to do. It's just one goal and you need to do it over and over in every piece of marketing. Let's break down that goal to make it clear:

- Your ***funnel*** is basically just a map of the relationship you have with an audience (that audience might be motivated sellers or cash buyers or any other audience you might choose to work with).
- ***Nurturing*** people through the funnel means building a relationship with them to move them through your funnel.
- And, you want ***more of the right people*** going through your funnel instead of the same number of people (a stagnant business) or the wrong people (which will just waste your time).

So, your overall marketing goal is to nurture more of the right people through your funnel; that means you need to find the very best audience (based on your avatar) get more and more of them into your funnel, and then build a relationship with them so they do a deal with you.

This is something I often say: real estate investors aren't in the real estate business... they're in the people business. You're just finding people who you can help. You're the "middleman" (or woman) who finds a seller, adds value to the real estate, and then matches it up with a buyer or tenant. The real estate barely matters, actually! The bigger thing at work here is the relationships you build.

(Case in point: Several of my clients build a big cash buyers list and that allows them to do deals in any market! They focus on the relationship first, and then that gives them the power to choose the kinds of markets and deals they want to do.)

There are many real estate investors who focus on the wrong things in their business but if you work on nurturing more of the right people through your funnel, you will build a strong and growing and profitable business that lasts a long time.

Make this goal your most important goal every day: to nurture more of the right people through your funnel.

Your List Is The Most Important Thing

If you're wondering how to nurture more of the right people through the funnel, it comes down to this: you are building a list of people and then you are building a relationship with the people on that list.

The bigger the list, and the stronger your relationship with them, the more deals you can do. (Actually, you'll probably have multiple lists—at least one for sellers and at least one for buyers.)

One of my clients has secretly built one of the largest lists of cash buyers I have ever seen and I joke with him that if his house burned to the ground, he would rush in and save his list. (Of course that's a joke because he doesn't keep it on a piece of paper... but it illustrates just how important his list is.)

So, every day you should wake up and ask yourself how you can add more names to your lists and how you can build a stronger relationship with that list.

Just to make this actionable, let me make this recommendation: Get a notebook. Open up the first page. Put today's date at the top. Then draw this chart:

	Seller List	Buyer List
How To Build The List		
How To Deepen The Relationship		

Then make it a goal to write an action in each square of the chart, and then implement. For example, you might write ideas like:

Of course there are many other ideas but you might write one of those ideas in each box of the chart and work on that until you've accomplished it.

Then? Turn the page of your notebook, draw the chart again, and make it a goal to think of new actions you can put in each square.

(Need a fast place to start? I'll give you some specific marketing ideas in an upcoming chapter and they can be the things you fill in early on!)

Some ideas will be duds. Others will be winners. Some will be big ideas. Others will be refinements of an idea that is already working.

For example, you might write:

	Seller List	Buyer List
How To Build The List	Split test postcards	Write a book
How To Deepen The Relationship	Use the person's name more often when talking to them	Get more testimonials from past buyers

See how this works? You're forcing yourself to create new ideas every day and push yourself to constantly grow your list while keeping your main goal (of nurturing more of the right people through your funnel) as the front-and-center activity you do.

The end result is only good things for your business! While your competitive investors are busy chasing the gurus to try copycat strategies that may or may not work where they are doing business, you are simply focused on the one and only thing that really matters in your business.

Do this, and everything else will take care of itself.

That's It?

Yes. Were you expecting more? You reached the end of the chapter and were hoping that I'd say: "send this many postcards and you'll do this many deals; then send this specific email to buyers and you'll definitely move those wholesale contracts!"

We'll get to the more practical stuff next but we needed to help you take a more strategic approach to your marketing first!

By the way, if you have marketing copy that you're already using in your business and you just want to see if there's a way to get it converting at a higher level for you then visit the link below to book a copy critique. Many investors book a copy critique to get a professional opinion of their existing marketing (plus a ton of insight about how to improve it!)
RealEstateInvestingCopywriter.com/copycritique

PART 4: CREATE AND DEPLOY YOUR MARKETING

Let me guess: You turned here first, right? You picked up this book, flipped past chapters 1 through 10, and landed here.

I'm guessing you did that because everything before this seemed high-level and strategic while part 4 looked like it was tactical and for action-takers. And maybe you were thinking, "this is a marketing book but we don't seem to get to marketing until part 4?!?!"

Well, hold on. Let's get a few things straight: it's ALL marketing that you're doing all the way back to Chapter 1. And many investors skip the pieces outlined in Parts 1, 2, and 3… which makes the actual marketing activities much less effective and much more expensive.

Do those foundational parts first and then dig into what we cover in Part 4—the practical, tactical, actionable marketing stuff. While this entire book is focused on roll-up-your-sleeves action, it's the stuff in Part 4 that will get you moving forward with actually putting lead-generating marketing content out into the world so that your phone will start ringing.

By the end of Part 4 you will have a solid, clear marketing plan put together that you can get ready to deploy.

CHAPTER 11: DIFFERENT TYPES OF MARKETING AND HOW TO USE THEM

Now let's roll up our sleeves and start looking at the exact marketing that you need to do.

If you've gone through all the chapters above then the information in this chapter will be clear and straightforward and you should be able to see how it plugs into your sales funnel to serve your business!

I have three challenges in creating this chapter and I need to make you aware of them before we get into the details:

1. **This information is time-sensitive.** The market is always shifting and there could be things that are working right now but may change in the future. (A few years ago, Facebook would not have been on this list but it is now. Or another example: I'm not a fan of Twitter for most real estate investors but Twitter may change to become a really valuable for investors.) I have shared what I believe will work in the next 3-5 years but I'm always sharing updated ideas and strategies for people who have joined my VIP list (at RealEstateInvestingCopywriter.com/join) so make sure you're a VIP to stay up-to-date.
2. **This information is high-level.** It will vary slightly from one business to another and one market to another. A rehabber may find one combination of these marketing tactics more useful than others, while a wholesaler may find a different combination of marketing tactics. I don't know your business model or sales funnel so I'm giving the best high-level version that you should start with, then build from there.
3. **This information is a starting point.** I would love to provide you with a step-by-step tutorial on how to really master each one of these marketing strategies. But *that* book would be 1,000 pages long and I'd never finish writing it because by the time I got to page 900, I'd need to go back and revise steps and screenshots because there was a change or update. So I'm only providing you with a starting point in this list below—a "shortlist" of tactics as a starting point that you can build on. If you're going to learn to do it yourself, use this list a "curriculum" so you know what information

to study and what information to ignore. If you're going to outsource your marketing, use this list as a way to find the best people to delegate to.

There are three different aspects of your business that you may need or want to market. Read them all below and decide which ones apply to your business.

- The seller side of your business
- The buyer side of your business
- Your umbrella business

You'll also notice that I've divided each section up into **Must-Haves** and **May-Wants**. The Must-Haves are things you really need right now. The May-Wants are things you might consider later. (If it's not on the list, you may want to test it to see if it's right for you but you may not need it.)

The Seller Side Of Your Business

As I often say, investors are one of the only industries where you have to *sell* in order to get inventory so that you can then sell it to a buyer! I can't think of another business that does this! While there are some exceptions, many investors I talk to need to find properties through marketing and then *sell* their services to the seller to convince them to sell. So, what do you need to market to sellers in your business?

Must-Have: If it's motivated sellers you're after, I've yet to see a better method of finding motivated sellers than **direct mail**—postcards, letters, or "Yellow Letters" are the most commonly used. This is so measurable, which makes it powerful: you can send out 1,000 of one type of postcard and 1,000 of another type of postcard and you'll know within a week or two which postcard resulted in the most replies and which resulted in the best deals. (Pro tip: the most replies does not always result in the best deals.)

Many investors have success with **bandit signs**, and I love them because of their simplicity. You may want to watch where you put your bandit signs, though, because some investors get lazy and just put out signs in clumps with other investors' signs; plus, there could be municipal laws that you want to be aware of (even if you strategically choose to ignore them—which I'm *not* advising you to do but telling you that many investors decide that the reward is greater than the fine they have to pay).

I also recommend a **website**. Some investors don't use a website to attract sellers but I think it's a great idea because it has a two-fold effect: for sellers who are searching online, it's a way for them to find you. And, for those who are already interacting with you, it's a way for them to research you and discover your credibility. Your website should include a **blog** where you can write articles, upload testimonials and case studies, and more.

I also recommend **video**. Video is a great way to attract sellers and connect with them, and it's often under-used by most investors (which means you can get some great search engine traffic from video because no one else is doing it!) Keep it simple with a YouTube channel and videos recorded from your phone.

Depending on who your motivated sellers are and where you connect with them, you may also want some other material. For example, I have some clients who find a lot of absentee owner motivated sellers (burnt out landlords!) at their local Real Estate Investing Associations (REIA) so I recommend having a simple **educational brochure (which also functions as a marketing and sales piece!)** that communicates what you do. If you end up interacting in person with sellers then you may want this as well. And, if you have relationships with referral partners who may refer sellers to you then a version of this kind of brochure may be valuable there too.

Once you've done all this marketing to find sellers, they'll want to reach out and ask you questions and see if you can help them. Therefore, you should also have some copy prepared for your voicemail, as well as **phone scripts** or **word tracks for text messages** for anyone on your team who answers the phone or calls back those who leave messages.

As you interact with these sellers, you will likely need more marketing material like **educational material** to help them choose you as the person to buy their house.

May-Want: You may want a few other things. A **Facebook page** might be a good way to advertise to potential sellers. **Instagram** has some potential here too, especially in the next few years, and especially if you master hashtags. You may also want to experiment with **print advertising in local newspapers**, but this should be tested.

Of course there are other things that you may want eventually—from **print marketing** that you can give out to people you meet, or even fancy **car wraps**. But don't jump on these last two tactics just yet until you've got everything in place and working well.

The Buyer Side Of Your Business

I work with real estate investors of every type and business model, who have different needs for finding buyers. One client, John, uses a fairly traditional approach to market his rehabbed homes to retail buyers. Another client, Mark, uses online marketing to build a list of cash-paying investors to buy his turnkey properties. Another client, Frank, doesn't do a lot of marketing on the buyer side because he sells to a combination of friends, family, and hedge funds. While most investors come to me because they're looking for motivated sellers, many investors have many different goals to find buyers. So I'm sharing below what works most of the time but you may find that your specific niche needs something or something less... but start here.

Must-Have: Get a **website**. You'll want to use it to introduce yourself and build credibility. Since you're asking people to give you their money, you'll want to build a lot of credibility! Your website should also include a **blog** so that you can post valuable information, testimonials and case studies, and more.

You'll also want a way to capture information so that you can build a relationship with prospective clients. **Email marketing** is a great way to do that. Sign up for an email marketing system, put an email capture form on your website, and get people to add their emails to get more information and great deals from you. (Even if you aren't marketing to buyers—perhaps because you're like my client Frank who doesn't need buyers—you can still use email marketing to maintain the relationship with your existing investors or to build for a future when you might need buyers or when you might want to sell something else to those buyers.)

One great way to find buyers and position yourself as an expert is to provide them with **educational material**. Teaching other people helps to position you as a credible and trustworthy authority, it builds loyalty, and (in some cases) you can sell some of your information for another stream of income. Your educational material can appear on your site, in blog posts, in your email (especially as an incentive to subscribe) and when you're asking investors to buy your deals.

You should also be producing video. **Video (on YouTube, Facebook, and Instagram), including Live Video,** is a powerful way to position yourself and create content. The great thing is, you can often repurpose this video—just record it once and upload it everywhere.

And, social media, especially **Facebook**, **LinkedIn**, and **Instagram**, are all Must-Have ways to build relationships with potential investors. Whether you use a corporate page or your own personal page is up to you and depends on your brand but you should at least be in these places.

This next one is big and it might take a while to create but you also need a **book**. Yes, I do think this is a Must-Have to get buyers. It doesn't have to be a big book but it needs to be a printed book that is for sale on Amazon. Why a book? Because with buyers, you are asking them to give you tens of thousands of dollars (or more), and you need a TON of credibility and trust in order for them to do that. A book is, in my opinion, the fastest way to create credibility and trust—and a lot of it!—for people who have money. A book looks like a super-scary, intimidating investment of time and money but it doesn't have to be. I write *a lot* of books for my clients and I've built a fun, simple, streamlined system to create a book fairly quickly.

May-Want: These May-Want options are really valuable and I work with a lot of investors who are killing it with some of these. However, they are not right for everyone (and they may also depend on how much time you have).

You may want to publish some of your blog posts elsewhere. I really like a **BiggerPockets blog** and **Medium.com** (and don't forget to post your blogs on Facebook and LinkedIn, too, of course!) BiggerPockets and Medium can sometimes be a little work intensive if you get a lot of comments but they can help to promote you so it could be worth it.

A **podcast** is another area that investors have a lot of opportunities with. Podcasts were big for a while, they declined in popularity for a bit, but now they are back in a very big way (and Gary Vaynerchuk thinks that audio and video, including podcasts, are the future of the internet). So, if you're not doing them, you should be doing them now. I've got a great contact who specializes in helping real estate investors start and promote their podcasts. We work together all the time and have helped several investors do this. I'll introduce you to this contact on my secret bonus page: RealEstateInvestingCopywriter.com/bonus/playbookbonus

Your Umbrella Business

No, this is not another line of business in which you sell umbrellas. Haha! Rather, it's the way a lot investors' businesses are structured, and if yours is structured this way then there may be a reason to market this part of your business as well.

For example, one common scenario that I see a lot is an umbrella LLC (let's call it: "Aaron Hoos Investments LLC") and underneath that you have two sides to your business—a seller side and a buyer side. These seller and buyer sides operate almost independently but all the money is transacted through "Aaron Hoos Investments LLC". (Note: I'm not giving you legal advice about how you should construct your business, I'm just telling you what is one way that I see a lot of investors structuring their business and I'm sharing my approach to how to market this.)

In these situations, the buyer side of the business and the seller side of the business are marketed independently of each other. And for a lot of investors, marketing the buyer side and the seller side is all you need to do.

However, for some investors, there may be a reason to market the larger company as well. Perhaps you sell products or services through that company, which is the case for a lot of my clients who start out doing one type of investing but end up bolting on different businesses and revenue streams, to the point where it makes sense to create and market a compelling umbrella brand.

So, marketing your umbrella brand is not necessary in the early days as long as you are focused on marketing to sellers and buyers. However, there may come a point in your business where it makes sense to market this. If this is the case for you, here is what I advise:

Must-Have: At the very least, you should consider a **website**. It can be a very simple website, that links to your seller and buyer sites. In my experience you probably won't market this site very often. Rather, it's there to give you further credibility (especially to cash buyers who want to know more about you) as well as a convenient way to show how your business is organized. As you grow, you can add pages to display other products and services and lines of business.

May-Want: If you are growing this umbrella part of your business intentionally then you could probably use branded content like **business cards** and perhaps an **Instagram** account if you want to display your brand, products, and happy customers. A **LinkedIn business profile** and a **Facebook page** may work in your situation too.

Frequently, that's all you'll need unless you are actively selling products and services from this umbrella site, when you may want other things too like **Facebook ads** and **email marketing**.

Summary

These are the basic types of marketing that you Must-Have and May-Want in your real estate investing business.

When you start your real estate investing business, you should focus on the Must-Haves. Don't worry about the May-Wants for now. Just get those Must-Haves dialed in to your sales funnel, fill in any gaps that are missing (since every investor's sales funnel will be unique) and then work on them until they are working successfully for you. Test them. Modify them. Analyze them.

THE REAL ESTATE INVESTING COPYWRITER'S PLAYBOOK

Eventually, you'll be ready to move to the May-Wants and see what could work to take your business to the next level (but don't rush into these until your Must-Haves are dialed in.)

Over time, this list will change as technology and user trends change. So, you'll want to make sure you are connected with me on my VIP email list because I'll keep you up-to-date there with some of the latest opportunities that my clients are using well. You can join my VIP email list at: RealEstateInvestingCopywriter.com/join

---

Last minute edit: I'm not exaggerating about the ever-evolving list. The list will change... *a lot*. In fact, in the months it took me to write this book, the list changed a few of times. As I'm going to print, it's continuing to change: Instagram TV is a new thing. I'm paying attention to Facebook because of recent political and legal issues they've run into (I'm not worried about them shutting down, and the "Must-Haves" above continue to be true; I've updated them just before going to print.) Podcasts are coming back after a few years of being less popular. I'm seeing shifts in the times of day that people consume social media content.

... Heck, I'm even paying attention to what some people are doing on Tinder to sell things! (Yes, there are salespeople on Tinder who have set up profiles and convert swipers into customers... maybe you'll be the first real estate investor on Tinder to find sellers or buyers?!?)

So I urge you to get over to RealEstateInvestingCopywriter.com/join and make sure you have joined my VIP list to get the latest information on the very best strategies, methods, media, and marketing channels.

That VIP list is also a great place to tell me about yourself and where you are doing deals, and I often follow-up with people and try to make introductions and connections if I think there is a fit among people... whether it's another investor doing business in the area, or a podcaster looking for a guest, or whatever! I love introducing people who can work together! So join the VIP list at:

RealEstateInvestingCopywriter.com/join

CHAPTER 12: THE SCIENCE OF COPYWRITING

When I say "copywriting" what do you think of?

Some people mistake it for "copyright" (which is the legal right of ownership by a content creator) and a lot of people think of copywriting as merely writing words for marketing purposes. But there's more to it than that. Someone who writes well isn't automatically a copywriter; even someone who writes marketing content well isn't necessarily a copywriter.

People who don't spend a lot of time in the world of marketing and copywriting may think of it as an art (perhaps like many other types of writing)... as if copywriting was something mysterious and open to interpretation. But one of the things that I love about copywriting is that it's not really an art at all; copywriting is a science.

You see, science is about making the unknown known, and turning it into a predictable sequence that works every time. For example, when you turn the temperature down to a certain point, water will freeze. When you turn the temperature up to a certain point, water will boil. Science has revealed the predictable reality of temperature's effect on water, and it works over and over, every single time (with few exceptions based on your altitude, the purity of the water, etc.).

Copywriting is a science for similar reasons. It follows a very specific step-by-step sequence and relies on the right ingredients, and when those things come together, the copywriting will work predictably.

It's a science honed from years of study—not just the 20+ years I've put into studying copywriting but into the more-than-a-century that has gone into studying the science of copywriting, and thousands of years of the study of human psychology (upon which all copywriting is built).

Why am I telling you this? Well, because I want to give you the exciting news: if you want to get better at growing your real estate investing business then one of the best things you can do is to become familiar with copywriting, and either hone your copywriting skills or work with someone who does.

What Is Copywriting?

Copywriting is *selling with words*. That is the most important concept to remember.

Unlike other types of marketing copy (including most blog posts and the content on your website), which is "telling," copywriting is selling. Copywriting compels the reader to take a specific action, whatever it is you want them to do, and it should sell the reader on taking the next action *with you*.

For example, the copywriting on a postcard should sell a motivated seller to pick up the phone and call you; the copywriting on a website should sell a cash buyer to enter their information so they can get great cash-flowing deals from you; the copywriting inside an educational handout should sell a motivated seller on allowing you to put their house under contract; the copywriting in a deal email should sell a cash buyer on why they should click the reply button to acquire your latest wholesale deal; the copywriting on an event brochure should sell an investor on why they should attend your investing event.

Copywriting should sell the reader on taking the next action, whether that action is a small step to get in touch or it's the final step to do a deal. Think of your sales funnel, which we covered in an earlier chapter: there are multiple steps in the sales funnels that your sellers or buyers follow as they interact with your business. Every single touchpoint likely requires some form of copywriting in order to move them in steps down your sales funnel—for example:

1. Your postcard to a seller should be written with strategic copywriting to convince the seller to call you.
2. When they call, the words you say to the seller (the "script") should be written with strategic copywriting to convince the seller to set an appointment for an offer (if that's what your business model is).
3. When you're face-to-face with the seller, you'll probably want some supporting documentation (including brochures and a script) that is written with strategic copywriting to convince the seller to accept your offer.

That's why some investors even hire me to write out the sales scripts that their virtual assistants will use when those assistants answer phone calls.

Why Is Copywriting Important?

Chances are, you're reading this book because you know the importance of copywriting. That's the case for most investors who get in touch with me: they discover that just "regular marketing writing" (which is unmeasurable and not easily testable) is not the preferred approach so they seek me out to apply a copywriting approach to the content in their sales funnel. But just in case you don't know why copywriting is important, let me get you up to speed: copywriting is important because it is a science. It turns the unexpected into the predictable: *if your copywriting compels people to act, it worked. If it doesn't compel people to act, it doesn't work. Period.* And what makes copywriting important is: you can understand the science of copywriting to understand what makes it work (or not work), and how to make it increasingly effective each time you use it.

Copywriting uses a specific group of components: Thousands of years ago, an ancient person might have told you that fire was a magical gift from the gods; it existed or didn't exist because of the whims of divine beings. But science knows that there are three components to make fire: oxygen, heat, and fuel. Those are proven ingredients. And any time you want fire, you need those three things.

Likewise, with copywriting, there are proven ingredients that are combined together to compel the reader to act. (I'll cover the ingredients shortly—keep reading). Good copywriters know the ingredients and work to combine them together as effectively as possible to create results.

Copywriting arranges those components in a specific way to elicit an action: Just because you have the right ingredients doesn't mean you automatically have effective copy. Those ingredients need to be combined together in the right way.

Think of your kitchen: you probably use a few similar ingredients to make a variety of food. Just a small change in what you do, when, and what small things you add, will work together to create completely different meals.

Likewise, with your copywriting, you use the right ingredients but you use them in a very specific and strategic way, depending on what point in the sales funnel your audience is and what you want them to do. I'll show you a really powerful strategy in the next chapter for that!

Copywriting uses scientific testing: If you just sat down and wrote out a marketing piece, such as your website or a postcard, then you sat back and monitored results, you might not know why those things did or didn't work, or what you could do to improve it. And if you tried to improve it, the changes would largely depend on how you felt about it at the time.

I come back to the idea of copywriting as a science because it also takes a scientific approach to testing: an inexperienced marketer would write one postcard and send it out, then write a completely different postcard the next time and send it out… and they would end up confused about why one works and one doesn't; meanwhile, an experienced marketer would write one postcard and then use a scientific method to figure out how to improve the results of that postcard each and every time.

The Root Of Copywriting

Copywriting is a science because it is measurable and testable. But it also has its root in another kind of science: human psychology.

Great copywriters may not necessarily be great writers (surprise!) but they are avid students of human psychology. Put two people in a room—a person who can write grammatically correct sentences and a person who loves psychology—and I would hire the person who loves psychology to do my copywriting for me.

The reason is: people don't take action for logical reasons. We actually take action for emotional reasons... and then back it up with logical ones. Your sellers make emotional decisions; your buyers make emotional decisions; you make emotional decisions; I make emotional decisions.

Yes, even you. Your house, your car, your career choice, your spouse, your clothes, your food, your vacation... even the flavor of gum you chew. Whether big decisions or little ones, whether permanent or short term, we all make decisions based on our emotions (even if we think we're making decisions based on logic)... then we justify our emotional decisions with logical ones.

Before buying a car, did you sit down and compare two similar cars and weigh them based on equivalent factors? Few people do but even if you did, you already were making emotional decisions in your head and that weighing-the-facts was just an exercise of justification.

That's why psychology is such an important field of study for copywriters: psychology is the study of how people think and act, while copywriting is all about getting people to take action. That's why I like to think of copywriting as *applied psychology* because copywriting is about understanding people's thinking so you can "hack into their brains" with psychological strategies and compel them to take action.

That's what it's all about: getting people to take action. Therefore, if you mastery psychology and how people think and act (and especially what motivates them to act) then you will create a stronger investing business that really nails the marketing, sales, and copywriting pieces because you get more people to act.

(That's also what makes me uniquely qualified to be a copywriter. People are surprised to learn that my educational background is not in journalism or English or writing. While my Master's degree was in business and strategy, my undergrad degree included studies in psychology and counseling. Even though they weren't my majors, I have come to rely on those studies daily to make my copywriting more effective, and have continued to invest heavily in further psychological studies throughout my career to make sure that I know what makes people's minds "tick.")

Having said all of this, I should also point something out here because I know I'll hear about if I don't: this sounds unethical—to hack someone's brain to get them to take action. The thing is: nearly all professional marketers and copywriters do it. If you've ever seen a commercial for McDonald's or Apple, it happened to you. So I will make it as plain as day: the onus is on marketers to choose to be ethical about their use of psychological hacks in copywriting. There will be unethical people using this information (and they would have used these strategies whether they read them here or somewhere else) but it's up to you to continue carefully selecting which sellers and buyers you want to work with and what services or solutions you have to offer them. There's nothing wrong with psychological hacking when it is ethically done with the underlying desire to help people.

And that's what it's all about: leveraging psychology in copywriting to help people (while getting a fair reward for that help). So, master psychology and you'll grow your investing business.

Want to learn more? I have a ton of resources about psychology on my blog (RealEstateInvestingCopywriter.com/blog) and on my VIP email list (RealEstateInvestingCopywriter.com/join) to those are good places to start.

I've also included a brief introduction to one of the most important fundamentals of psychology that will impact all of your copywriting. Study this and use it to craft the most effective copy…

The Psychology Of Motivation

A great copywriter should always be asking: "Why do people do what they do?" And then follow up with: "How can I get them to do what I want them to do?" Those are the foundational questions that underpin all of copywriting. If you can figure out what motivates your prospect to act then you can use that as a tool to persuade them.

And before we can get to the actual motivation part, we have to dig into the brain a little bit. You might be surprised at how we make decisions: you see, we humans think we are a pretty sophisticated bunch. We're riding around in self-driving cars, we're talking on phones that have more power than the technology that got the first men to the moon, and we're clicking our way to riches and success on the internet. It's a great time to be alive.

But when you strip it all away, guess what: we're not all that different from our ancient ancestors. We still need to eat, we still try to protect ourselves, we still have primal urges to procreate. Sure, it looks quite different now but we are doing the same things. We are ultimately still the same old primitive cave dwellers who are doing our best to mate with someone else while avoiding being eaten by wild animals. Put down your iPhone for a moment and go back in time to your ancient ancestors... because your brain really isn't any different.

Marketers and copywriters call it "the lizard brain" as a tongue-in-cheek way of saying that our basic ways of thinking is no different than the dinosaurs.

Although we like to think that we make informed decisions based on the compared features between two homes or cars or mobile devices, we are ultimately guided by our lizard brain.

And what does our lizard brain think about doing? Basically the lizard brain is the part of our brain responsible for keeping us alive and procreating. And it guides all of our decisions.

When faced with danger, our lizard brain commands us to fight or flee (depending on the danger); when faced with food, our lizard brain commands us to eat; when faced with a potential mate, our lizard brain tells us to preen and boast and flirt... all to feed the primal drives of survival (as individuals and as a species).

While you may not like reading that as a modern human, or as a consumer, this should be very good news to you as an investor who needs to market for more sellers and buyers. The reason is: you only need to hack into the person's lizard brain to get them to take action... and yes, this applies even if you are buying houses from motivated sellers or selling wholesale contracts or cash-flowing properties to cash buyers! Their lizard brains guide them to take action to sell to you or to buy from you (if you know how to hack into their brain).

So, how do you hack into their lizard brain to get people to take action? You'll love this useful tool I've developed...

It's a 2x2 matrix, creating 4 possible motivations. The first set of two motivations is well known and heavily reference by Tony Robbins. It's the idea that the underlying drivers in people's lives is to do one of the following:

- Pursue pleasure
- Avoid pain

At first glance, this seems to be more in line with the lizard brain that is getting us to fight, flee, eat, or procreate. They are all about pursuing pleasure or avoiding pain.

However, if we pause for a moment and consider our own lives or the people we know, it's more complicated than those two simple points above. For example: there are scenarios when people choose the more painful approach. In fact, you've probably met many sellers who chose not to take your simple offer because they thought they could get more their property by selling in a painful way on the market. And, you've probably met buyers who claimed to want to invest and had the money to do so but continued to invest in poorer-performing investments.

I used this Pleasure/Pain motivation set for a few years but was never happy with the reality that sellers and buyers sometimes made decisions that weren't obviously about avoiding pain or pursuing pleasure.

Then I realized what was missing: Yes, two of the motivations are pursuing pleasure and avoiding pain but those are also done in relation to two other motivations:

- Preservation (ensuring their survival)
- Position (enhancing their social status)

What that means is: people are motivated to **preserve** themselves (physically and emotionally), their families, their peace-of-mind, their social status, their financial status, etc. They want to remain in a sort of "protective stasis". And, people are also motivated to increase their **position**, including their social status, their bragging rights, their physical and financial realities, etc.

Together, these four motivations in a 2x2 chart, became my Real Estate Investing Copywriter's Motivation Quadrant™, and this unlocked the motivation puzzle for me.

	Avoid Pain	**Pursue Pleasure**
Preservation	People make decisions to avoid pain while preserving their situation	People make decisions to pursue pleasure while preserving their situation
Position	People make decisions to avoid pain while enhancing their social position	People make decisions to pursue pleasure while enhancing their social position

Let's look at this practically from a real estate investor's perspective when dealing with sellers:

	Avoid Pain	Pursue Pleasure
Preservation	Sellers may choose to sell to you because they are burnt out and sick of spending money on their money pit of a property and they just need to get rid of it.	Sellers may choose to sell to you to put cash in their pocket and pursue other opportunities.
Position	Sellers may choose to sell to you because they want to protect their social position so they will sell in a fast, private way (instead of listing their house, which might invite questions about why they are selling).	Sellers may choose to sell to you if they are frustrated with the bank and don't want to deal with them anymore... and want to be able to tell get the satisfaction of telling the banker to go screw themselves.

These are just a few examples of the many types of sellers and what their motivations are. Of course there are also negative examples, too, of sellers who choose NOT to do something for one or more of those reasons.

Now buyers:

	Avoid Pain	Pursue Pleasure
Preservation	Buyers may choose to buy a cash-flowing property because they haven't saved for retirement and they don't know how else they'll afford retirement.	Buyers may choose to flip a house because they need money and this looks like a fast, simple way to make the money they need.
Position	Buyers may choose to buy cash-flowing properties because they think the stock market is going to crash and they want a place to invest that will allow them to still boast about their returns while their friends struggle.	Buyers may choose to invest in a cash-flowing property because they want to be able to boast to their coworkers that they make extra money on the side and can quit anytime.

Again, these are just some example motivations of the many types of buyers you'll meet. Not only that, but there are also reverse motivations as well, where people choose not to do something for one or more of those reasons.

Take the time to understand this quadrant because when you do, you'll create better copy (and can even use it in your sales efforts too). And if you ever lose a deal? Go back to this quadrant and consider whether someone was motivated in a way that you just didn't realize at the time. A classic example that I see among investors is: talking to buyers the opportunity to get a better return on their investing dollars (that's a pleasure/preservation motivation) when many buyers are really about protecting their money (that's a pain/preservation motivation) or bragging to their friends (that's a pleasure/position motivation).

This is a powerful tool for copywriters because it forces you to drill down and get an answer from all relevant angles to the most important question, Why do people do what they do?

To use this chart, consider the copywriting that you are writing (A postcard? An email?) and who you are writing to (A seller? A buyer?). Then, consider what their motivations are. There are many buyers with many motivations but you might be able to either make some general assumptions based on who you are writing to, or, if you have the space, you can write to all four of the motivations for sellers or all four of the motivations for buyers.

For example, if it were me, here's what I would do with a couple pieces in my investing business:

- On a website that I was writing to buyers, I would aim to connect with all four of motivations, attempting to address the pain/preservation, pleasure/preservation, pain/position, pleasure/position points in the quadrant.
- In a postcard that I was writing to sellers, I would try to make some educated guesses about who my audience is and what they want or don't want. A burnt out landlord, for example, is probably motivated by preservation and avoiding pain; someone going through foreclosure may be motivated by preservation and avoiding pain, or, they may be motivated by position and pleasure if they think that selling their house to you will allow them to tell the bank to go screw themselves.

When copywriting, your job is to identify the motivations of the audience and then speak to those motivations to inspire your audience to take the appropriate action. Fortunately, it's not guesswork. You already know many of the motivations that your sellers or buyers possess (or you can make an educated guess at them), and you can always refine them over time.

Want to take fast action on this? Start by creating the chart that I've shown you in this chapter, and then filling it out for each different type of audience you have. (For example, if you serve burnt out landlords and sellers in foreclosure then you'll want to do a chart for each of those sellers… as well as a chart for each of your buyers.) Don't rush through this exercise because the better you understand and master your audiences' motivations, the better you'll do at getting them to take action.

Connecting Motivations To Copy

You've just read about motivations, but the question is: how do you write in a way that addresses their motivation?

I use a simple acronym to help me. (Remember this acronym because it will be important in the very next chapter!) I use the acronym **TRUE**, which is an acronym I developed from well-known copywriting components, to help me turn motivation with actions.

TRUE stands for:

- **T = Trust**—how you get the reader to believe you
- **R = Return on Investment (ROI)**—tells the reader how they will benefit
- **U = Urgency**—encourages the reader to act quickly
- **E = Engagement**—keeps the reader's eyes locked on your copy

If you want to get someone to take action, you need to find their motivation and then speak/write/connect with them and communicate these four things.

It works like this…

Motivation	The "TRUE" Bridge	Action

How is your audience motivated (use the chart from earlier in this chapter)	>>> Trust >>>
	 >>> ROI >>>
	 >>> Urgency >>>
	 >>> Engagement >>>
		What specific action do you want them to take?

When you know your audience's motivation, and the action you want them to take, then you communicate to build trust, establish ROI, incite urgency, and with engagement; those four components are the bridge between motivation and action.

Here's a non-investing example that I like to use because it's familiar to a lot of people: let's say you are with a bunch of friends and you're trying to decide what restaurant to eat at. You really want your friends to eat the restaurant of your choice. So, how do you take their motivation (of wanting to eat) and get them to take action by choosing the restaurant of your choice? You unconsciously use these four elements to convince them:

Trust: You might point out that you are all friends and you know them well, and you have personally chosen great restaurants in the past.

Return On Investment: You might point out that the restaurant's food it delicious and has great value, no matter what everyone's budget is, plus the seating is comfortable and not too loud so you can all enjoy each other's company.

Urgency: You might point out that everyone is hungry and needs to decide soon, plus tonight there's a special on appetizers.

Engagement: And of course you're not going to tell this to your friends in a quiet voice from the corner of the room; you will be animated and enthusiastic, and you might try to paint a picture of the restaurant's atmosphere and delicious food.

That illustrates how you took their motivation and then used four key components (based on the acronym TRUE) to convince them to choose your preferred restaurant to eat at.

The same thing happens with your investing audiences (sellers, buyers, etc.) when you are communicating to them through words, video, voicemail, or in person.

So, identify your audiences' motivations and the actions you want them to take, and then figure out what you need to say to them to build trust, establish ROI, incite urgency, and communicate in an engaging way.

I'll show you how to use this acronym in the very next chapter to build really effective copy!

Summary

Do you want to get started in copywriting for your real estate investing business and become rapidly successful at it? It's simple: become a student of psychology. Figure out what motivates people and create copy that leverages those motivations to get them to take action. In the next chapter we'll look at how to take those motivations, along with everything else you've been learning in this book, and turn it into compelling copy that gets your prospects taking action and ultimately helps you do more deals.

CHAPTER 13: THE COPYWRITING POWER MATRIX

Copywriting is not just about putting words to paper or screen. Copywriting is *selling with words*. It's the science of selling with words in a predictable way that you can test and prove.

One of the ways that we can become predictably better at copywriting is by using a proven, reliable sequence to sell. In sales (and in copywriting) there is a sequence that you can use to increase the likelihood that people will take action. If the sequence is not followed, you lose potential responses; if the sequence is followed, you gain potential responses.

There are a few variations of this sequence. One well known variation of this sales/copywriting sequence was made famous in the movie *Glengarry Glen Ross* (one of my favorite movies!), in which Alec Baldwin's character talks about the acronym AIDA—Attention, Interest, Decision, Action. That's been a staple of sales—and copywriting—for years.

I used that sequence in my copywriting for a long time, first attempting to capture the attention of the right audience, then generating interest in the offer, then getting the reader to make a decision to move forward with the solution I was offering, and finally getting the reader to take action. It's a solid, dependable sequence that you should become familiar with if you haven't already.

However, as I actively sought to improve my copywriting skills, and deliver high value to my real estate investing clients (and higher response rates in the work I wrote for them) I realized that the AIDA sequence it was lacking something. For example, if I was teaching this to an investor, they might ask: "well, how do I get their attention?" or "how do I increase interest?" And, even within the AIDA sequence there are overlooked opportunities to make it more effective and compel more action. Plus, I wanted to make it user-friendly and (nearly) foolproof so anyone could use it and create a pretty solid piece of effective copy. I tested, adjusted, and refined my own sequence and today I use and teach something that I call the Real Estate Investing Copywriting Power Matrix™. It starts with the typical sales sequence (adapted from AIDA; you'll see elements of it in there) but takes it to the next level... *and* it makes it easier for you to write.

The first difference is: it's a Matrix, not just a sequence. The second difference is: it's made up of two acronyms that work very powerfully together. Here's how it works:

Introduction To The Real Estate Investing Copywriting Power Matrix™

Down the side of the Matrix are five letters that make up the word "HARPO". **HARPO** is adapted from AIDA (with a few modifications based on my own research).

- **H = Headline**—where you capture attention
- **A = Anxiety**—where you list the problems that the reader faces
- **R = Remedy**—where you explain the solution to the problems
- **P = Proof**—where you back up the solution
- **O= Opportunity**—where you tell the reader how to get the solution

So, **HARPO** appears down the side like this...

H				
A				
R				
P				
O				

This is a good basic sequence that works for just about anything, from a postcard that a wholesaler would mail to motived sellers to a full-blown presentation with PowerPoints and slick brochures that a developer would show to a pre-construction investor. Nearly everything you write (when you want someone to take action) should follow this outline. Even something as short as a tweet can have this compressed down into just a few characters while something as long as a book can expand the HARPO sequence out to many chapters.

HARPO is just the start, though. If you used just this part of the sequence, you'd do okay but you may not create the most compelling copy possible. That's where the other acronym comes in...

Along the top of the Matrix are four letters that spell the word "TRUE", which I introduced to you in the last chapter. **TRUE** is the components that you need in every piece of copy to bridge from motivation to action. TRUE stands for...

- **T = Trust**—how you get the reader to believe you
- **R = Return on Investment (ROI)**—tells the reader how they will benefit
- **U = Urgency**—encourages the reader to act quickly
- **E = Engagement**—keeps the reader's eyes locked on your copy

So, **TRUE** appears across the top like this...

	T	R	U	E
H				
A				
R				
P				
O				

Each of these TRUE components need to appear in your copy (and the more they appear, the better).

Now let's look at these two acronyms together. The best way to understand how these two acronyms work together is to think of a recipe you may have used in the kitchen. TRUE is your list of ingredients; HARPO is the steps you use to put these ingredients together.

So, every investor who wants to write something that compels a seller or buyer (or some other client) to take action, should start with a Matrix that looks like this...

	T	R	U	E
H				
A				
R				
P				
O				

What's happening here is that every element of your sales copy sequence (HARPO) needs to contain specific components (TRUE), and this Matrix gives you some direction and focus as you build those components into your sales copy, like this:

- H: The **Headline** will contain elements of **T**rust, **R**OI, **U**rgency, and **E**ngagement;
- A: The **Anxiety** section will contain elements of **T**rust, **R**OI, **U**rgency, and **E**ngagement;
- R: The **Remedy** section will contain elements of **T**rust, **R**OI, **U**rgency, and **E**ngagement;
- P: The **Proof** section will contain elements of **T**rust, **R**OI, **U**rgency, and **E**ngagement;
- O: The **Opportunity** section will contain elements of **T**rust, **R**OI, **U**rgency, and **E**ngagement.

That's powerful! This approach ensures that the most compelling elements of copy (the elements that get people to take action!) are threaded throughout every section of your copy. It forces you to make sure your copy is as compelling as possible and eliminates the potential that you might write some copy and think "oh, that's probably close enough."

Plus, it speeds up and simplifies the writing process! It allows you to spend more energy on creating effective copy than on guessing what you should say next or how you should say something.

(And, as an added bonus, this Matrix helps to direct your attention and focus as you write so that you avoid writer's block or a sense of overwhelm from staring at a blank page and wondering how to start.)

> **BONUS**: I've created a downloadable resource of this chart so you can print it and use it yourself:
> RealEstateInvestingCopywriter.com/bonus/playbookbonus

Before we look at the Copywriting Power Matrix in a step-by-step way, why don't I show you what one looks like in real life? That way, you have some context by seeing how I have personally created one, and what it looks like when finished.

How I Use The Real Estate Investing Copywriting Power Matrix™

Whenever I want to write something, I start with my Copywriting Power Matrix! (If you've ever hired me to write something, I've probably done exactly this method on your work!)

I usually create this Matrix on one of the whiteboards in my office because that gives me enough space to work with. In fact, I'll show you exactly how I do it on my whiteboard (just excuse the messy lines and less-than-studio-quality photography). I start by drawing out the Copywriting Power Matrix on my whiteboard...

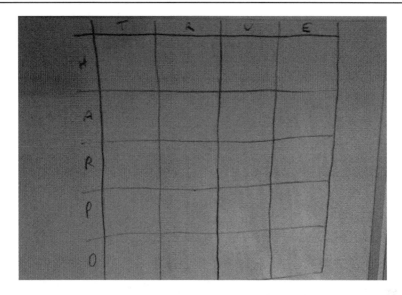

Once I have this Matrix drawn, I fill in each square with what I already know. I have the advantage of studying and writing for real estate investors for many years, so I'm now at a point where I can fill in quite a few squares right off the bat. (If you have even a couple of deals under your belt, you'll be able to fill in a few pieces on this Matrix too. If you're new to investing, it might take a little extra legwork and research but at least now your research is directed and focused!)

Here is what my whiteboard looks like as I build the content…

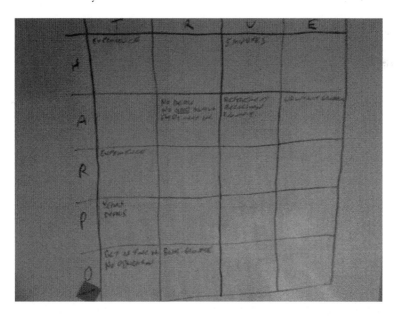

(Don't worry about the exact words that I've written in the squares in this example. Later in this chapter I'll show you exactly what you'll need to write in each square. I just want to show you the "big picture" of how this Matrix is created in real life.)

You'll see that I'm filling out the squares, plus I'm adding sticky notes on questions I have or angles I want to pursue. I continue doing this until I exhaust everything I know. You should never reach a point where you say "that's good enough; I can move on now… you should always write everything you can in each square.

At some point I will need to do some research (and you will too). When it's time to start researching, I research exhaustively to confirm the squares that I have filled out and to fill out squares that are still empty. I'll also include words or phrases that I think might connect with the audience, case studies and testimonials, numerical proof, etc.

By the end I have a chart that is jam packed with content. And when I have a lot of information, I start thinking about how to organize it (and even draw arrows to guide me).

Here's what a Copywriting Power Matrix looks like that is filled out, with arrows, although you may end up with much more content in each square. I'm just showing you a simple example here, with less content than usual so you can see how it all works, but I often have each square jammed with notes.

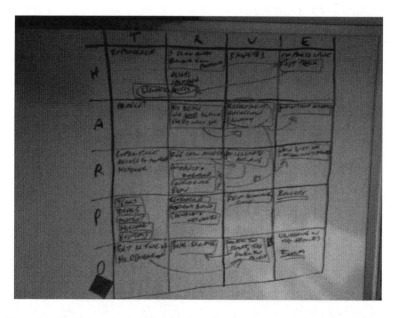

Once I've filled out the Matrix, I'm ready to start writing! I sit down at my computer and open up a Microsoft Word document (or wherever I'm creating the content) and then start at the top of the Matrix and literally just follow the arrows as I write.

By the end, I have a solid (but rough!) copy that goes through the HARPO sequence and contains all the components I need to motivate a reader to take action. Of course I'll still need to clean it up and I may need to adjust other pieces, but I'm 80%+ of the way there. The rest is just polishing, refining, and improving.

The example I've shown above was never intended to be shared (which is why the photographs are not great) but I just wanted to show you how it worked so you can go into the next section of this chapter with an idea of what it might look like when you're done.

Now let's go through each part of the Real Estate Investing Copywriting Power Matrix™ so you can see how it works. I'll go through the HARPO sequence first and then look at the TRUE components after.

Whenever you want to write something, just turn to this page of the book and go through each section of this chapter. There's power and value in having a template to go through. It makes your writing faster and simpler, and it ensures that you don't miss anything that could prevent you from doing more deals. Just as checklists can help you in other areas of your business, the Copywriting Power Matrix is like a checklist that ensures your copy is as compelling as it can be.

Therefore, one of the best ways to master the Copywriting Power Matrix and use it in your business is to read this chapter a couple of times and take notes in the area provided.

BONUS: Again, don't forget to get your own printable copy of this Copywriting Power Matrix so you can use it when creating your own marketing copy. Get it at:
RealEstateInvestingCopywriter.com/bonus/playbookbonus

I offer copywriting reviews and I use the Copywriting Power Matrix as my starting point when critiquing copy. Whether it's your copy or from another copywriter that you've hired, I'll run that copy through my Copywriting Power Matrix as a starting point. Get your copy critique here:
RealEstateInvestingCopywriter.com/copycritique

Copywriting Power Matrix—Headline (H)

The first part of the sales sequence that makes up the Copywriting Power Matrix is the **H**eadline.

	T	**R**	**U**	**E**
H	X	X	X	X
A				
R				
P				
O				

The purpose of the Headline section of the copy is to capture attention and to entice the reader to read more. You don't have to sell the entire solution in the headline; just get them to read more!

Our audiences are bombarded with information everywhere they turn so we need to create compelling (yet truthful!) headlines that stand out from the pack and demand to the reader to read OUR content instead of throwing out the mail or scrolling past our post.

I purposely used the word "headline" even though you might not always call it a headline in the writing you do. The label "headline" serves as a reminder that your copy should always have an attention-getting element to it, even if sometimes it's a headline and other times it is not. (For example, an email doesn't technically have a headline but its subject line serves the same purpose as a headline.)

Your headline is made up of the components **T**rust, **R**OI, **U**rgency, and **E**ngagement (you'll learn more about these shortly). Use as many of these as possible in your headline to create the most compelling headline that demands to be read.

Here are some tips to write a great Headline:

A sales letter usually has a headline. You've seen them on websites or perhaps in your mailbox. When you write sales letter headlines, keep them under 3 lines and make them big, if space permits.

A blog post has a headline too. It's often the title that you put at the top of your post. You can easily turn blog posts into copywriting by adding a strong headline at the top and a clear, simple call to action at the bottom of the post.

An email has a headline—usually the subject line. (Bonus tip: You can also increase open rates of your emails by making the very first line of your email an attention-getting headline. That's because many desktop and mobile device email interfaces will display the first few lines of an email, so it acts as a secondary headline.)

Your social posts don't have a separate headline section but you can increase readership if you make the first sentence an attention-getting headline in ALL CAPS, and it has the same function as a headline.

Keep headlines short, powerful, provocative, but always truthful. Don't try to squeeze all the benefits of your solution into your headline, just lead with the biggest, juiciest one. Be willing to shock people a little bit or tell a story if possible.

One of the most famous headlines in the history of copywriting tells a simple story in a single sentence as a very compelling headline: "***They all laughed when I sat down at the piano, but when I started to play!***" See how this headline is provocative, has a narrative quality to it, and also entices you to keep reading to find out what happened?

Use this space to write additional notes or ideas that apply to you:

_____
_____
_____
_____
_____
_____
_____
_____

Copywriting Power Matrix—Anxiety (A)

The second part of the sales sequence that makes up the Copywriting Power Matrix is the **A**nxiety section.

	T	R	U	E
H				
A	X	X	X	X
R				
P				
O				

The purpose of the Anxiety section is to highlight the pain that your reader is feeling about their situation, and to increase that feeling of pain to get them to take action. Many people feel anxiety and pain about many different things but often people learn to tolerate and live with these feelings, so you need to increase that feeling of pain to show that there is a painful cost to not taking action.

In sales letters and social posts, you can put this pain into one or more paragraphs. In shorter content, such as emails, use bullet points.

The Anxiety section is made up of the components **T**rust, **R**OI, **U**rgency, and **E**ngagement. Use as many of these as possible.

Here are some tips to write a great Anxiety section:

Don't hold back on the pain, and don't assume that your reader can draw all the conclusions that you do. If someone is going to lose their house, they may only be thinking of the anger they feel about having the bank take away their house, but you can highlight other things that they don't even realize are problems too, such as: the humiliation they may feel when someone asks them why they moved; the inconvenience of moving; the challenges their kids will have when trying to adjust to a new school; the lingering impact on their credit; the years of worrying that it might happen again; the loss of a home where they've built up memories with their family; the worries of maybe having to rent for a few years in a bad neighborhood; the loss of neighbors who have become friends; the feeling of throwing away money by renting (instead of owning); etc.

Most of the time you should talk about these anxieties in the form of "you", and try to paint a picture instead of simply reporting facts. For example: "Imagine how you'll feel when your kids come home with their eyes filled with tears; they miss their friends and this school isn't teaching the same things. They wish they could go back to their old school and hang out with their friends but they can't anymore because you're renting a home in a different school district."

Use this space to write additional notes or ideas that apply to you:

Copywriting Power Matrix—Remedy (R)

The third part of the sales sequence that makes up the Copywriting Power Matrix is the **R**emedy.

	T	R	U	E
H				
A				
R	X	X	X	X
P				
O				

The purpose of the Remedy section is to reveal that you have a solution to the reader's burning pain. Share what the solution is and how it benefits the reader.

This is the solution to the anxieties you have just listed in the previous part of your sales copy. In shorter copy (like emails or social posts) you can launch right into the solution; in longer copy (like sales letters or videos) you should talk about how you have a solution to the anxieties listed, and then talk about the solution.

The Remedy section is made up of the components **T**rust, **R**OI, **U**rgency, and **E**ngagement. Use as many of these as possible.

Here are some tips to write a great Remedy section:

If you addressed an item in your Anxieties section, you should show how the current solution addresses that specific anxiety. Do this for every anxiety you list.

A good remedy shouldn't just be the solution that you *do*, it should be an actual *thing*. You should productize your solution. So, one of the things I work with a lot of investors on is to take their solution ("we pay cash for your house") and turn it into a productized "thing" that seems more tangible. For example, when writing for clients who need copy to reach sellers, I often productize the investors' services with words like: "FastCash Sale™ System" or "Quick Move-Out™ Solution" (or a variation on those). When a seller has two nearly identical sales letters or postcards in their hands, but one of those has a solution called the "Quick Move-Out™ Solution" the seller is more likely going to choose that investor because it looks like it's a pre-built, laser-targeted solution.

SHORTCUT

Your productized solution doesn't have to be anything different than what you already do. You don't need to reinvent the wheel. All you are doing is applying a strategic name to an existing service to make it look like a pre-built package.

The truth is: it already IS a pre-built package but most investors don't perceive the value of their own services!

Simply list all the steps or solutions you have on a piece of paper, add the terminology at the top of the piece of paper, and you have created your solution. It's very simple.

Use this space to write additional notes or ideas that apply to you:
_____
_____
_____
_____
_____
_____
_____
_____
_____
_____

Copywriting Power Matrix—Proof (P)

The fourth part of the sales sequence that makes up the Copywriting Power Matrix is the **P**roof.

	T	R	U	E
H				
A				
R				
P	X	X	X	X
O				

The purpose of the Proof section is to assure the reader that your solution works and will work for them to help them solve the problem or challenge that they are facing.

Proof often includes things like facts and statistic, research, testimonials, case studies, endorsements, and demonstrations. These help to reinforce the reasons why someone would want your solution, and they put the seller or buyer at ease by showing that they are in good hands.

The Proof section is made up of the components **T**rust, **R**OI, **U**rgency, and **E**ngagement. Use as many of these as possible.

Here are some tips to write a great Proof section:

The very best source of proof is an unsolicited testimonial that gives a before and after word-picture of the situation, as well as a photo and the full name and contact information of the person who provided the testimonial. (Of course, you can't always get that but get as much as you can.) Another good testimonial is one recorded on video.

Unfortunately, most people forget to ask for testimonials or they are too scared to do so. To solve this, make it part of your process, as if every customer provides a testimonial at the end of receiving service from you, and simply ask: "would you prefer to write one or record one by video?" To make it even easier, write 3-5 testimonial templates that the seller can choose from and have them fill out the appropriate information and sign it.

If you are brand new to investing, or if you haven't done a great job of getting testimonials so far, that's okay. You can use the following strategies to provide proof:

- Use industry numbers (of course use them truthfully). For example, if you are a wholesaler and 5% of the people in your county sell through wholesalers, then say that. You're leveraging industry facts and statistics to position your service.
- Get endorsements from people who like you (even if they haven't done a deal with you.). For example, if you know a local celebrity, get them to write a brief endorsement that says, "If I needed help invest my money for cash flow, [your name] would be my very first call."

Make it a point to always be collecting proof elements whenever you can, and use as many as possible in your copywriting.

Use this space to write additional notes or ideas that apply to you:

Copywriting Power Matrix—Opportunity (O)

The fifth part of the sales sequence that makes up the Copywriting Power Matrix is the **O**pportunity.

	T	R	U	E
H				
A				
R				
P				
O	X	X	X	X

The purpose of the Opportunity section is to show the reader how to get the solution for themselves. Think of this as the call to action in which you specifically outline the steps they need to take to move forward.

For postcards that you send to motivated sellers, it might be your phone number. For an email you send to cash buyers, it might be a link they need to click. For your website, it might be a "subscribe now" button to join your email list.

The Proof section is made up of the components **T**rust, **R**OI, **U**rgency, and **E**ngagement. Use as many of these as possible.

Here are some tips to write a great Opportunity section:

A great opportunity section should have just one action for the person to take. In the list I gave above, you'll notice that I listed three different types of marketing (a postcard, an email, and your website) and you'll see that each of these has just one call to action.

Many eager investors try to squeeze more calls to action in on every piece of marketing but this is a mistake. When you provide your audience with too many choices, they won't choose; they'll get stuck. So, provide one clear and simple action for them to choose.

(The only exception to this would be a few pages on your website, such as your home page, where you might give readers several options to choose from—such as reading your blog, subscribing to your email newsletter, or contacting you. However, as people dig into your website and encounter more pages where you want them to take action, they should see only one action to take.)

Use this space to write additional notes or ideas that apply to you:

Copywriting Power Matrix—Trust (T)

The first part of the sales copy component that makes up the Copywriting Power Matrix is **T**rust.

	T	R	U	E
H	X			
A	X			
R	X			
P	X			
O	X			

Most people will only do business with you if they trust you. If they don't trust you, they most likely won't do business with you, or at least you will find it much harder to do business with them. As more and more investors enter the marketplace and compete with you to scoop up deals, more and more motivated sellers and cash buyers grow more sensitive, and more wary to the charlatans in the market.

Fortunately, there are many ways to build trust. Trust comes from rapport (seeking to understand your audience), credibility and authority (being a leader in your market), proactive value (providing something free early in the relationship), knowledge (teaching them something), and proof that you have helped other people (including testimonials). There are other ways to build trust too but these are a great start and easy for most investors to do.

Trust should be built all the way through your sales copy — in the **H**eadline, the **A**nxiety section, the **R**emedy section, the **P**roof section, and the **O**pportunity section.

Here are some tips to add Trust into your copy:

One of the simplest and fastest ways to build rapport is to know your audience's pain points and motivational drivers and articulate those. Your audience will unconsciously feel that you really understand them, and that is the basis of rapport. To do this well, read some of the earlier chapters in this book about identifying your target market and digging into their motivational psychology then make sure you write your copy in a way that demonstrates how much you understand.

Another very simple way to build trust for social media is to lead with educational value. Yes, you can do this in your sales copy! Create information that your audience needs to know and weave it into your content. A great example for sellers is a checklist-style resource that compares the benefits they get by selling to you versus selling the traditional way (through an agent on the market). And for buyers, you might create a checklist-style resource that compares the benefits of investing on the stock market versus investing in a cash-flowing property.

Use this space to write additional notes or ideas that apply to you:

Copywriting Power Matrix—ROI (R)

The second part of the sales copy component that makes up the Copywriting Power Matrix is the **R**eturn on investment (ROI).

	T	R	U	E
H		X		
A		X		
R		X		
P		X		
O		X		

When you ask someone to take action, you're asking them to trade something of theirs... maybe time or money or effort or even their reputation. They'll want to know if the trade will be worthwhile.

Therefore, you'll want to establish all the way through your copy that you deliver ROI—a return on whatever investment they will be making.

Remember that ROI is not always about money. Your sellers are "investing" in your ability to buy their house—the currency they're investing with is their trust and hope in you, as well as their credibility or financial credit (depending on their reasons for selling). And in return they're getting a future, peace-of-mind, less stress, etc.

Your buyers are investing money (and perhaps effort, their reputation, and more) to get a property that will provide a return of things like cash flow, early retirement, or even bragging rights among friends.

ROI should be built all the way through your sales copy — in the **H**eadline, the **A**nxiety section, the **R**emedy section, the **P**roof section, and the **O**pportunity section.

Here are some tips to add ROI into your copy:

Always remember that people aren't just investing money to get money. They invest a lot of things to get a lot of things, and it's rarely about money itself (but rather what the money can buy).

The best way to write a great ROI section throughout your copy is to pause every time you write about the return of time or money and try to drill down to the emotional benefit that they really get, and then (when possible) write it into a little story. So, a cash-flowing property isn't just about money in the bank every month, it's about escaping the soul-crushing daily commute and the feeling of finally screaming "screw you!" to your horrible boss as you leave the office for the last time.

It isn't always possible to create lengthy ROI stories but little emotional word-pictures that are peppered through your copy can be quite powerful.

Use this space to write additional notes or ideas that apply to you:

_____
_____
_____
_____
_____
_____
_____
_____
_____
_____
_____
_____
_____
_____
_____
_____
_____
_____
_____

Copywriting Power Matrix—Urgency (U)

The third part of the sales copy component that makes up the Copywriting Power Matrix is the **U**rgency.

	T	R	U	E
H			X	
A			X	
R			X	
P			X	
O			X	

Even though people feel a lot of pain about the challenges in their life, and even though the return on investment may be worth it, people don't like change. They fear it. They avoid it. Many people prefer the stasis of pain to the growth of change, even if it means continuing in a negative and challenging situation! So your copy needs to highlight why they need to act today to solve the problem.

Even those who know they need to make a change and take action may be inclined to put off the action for another day under the guise of "wanting to think about it" (without realizing that this "wanting to think about it" is just a delaying tactic to avoid change).

You should build urgency throughout your copy because people need to be reminded to act today. The urgency can be based on some factor outside of your control (such as: the first person to tell me they want this cash-flowing *and* send the money gets this property); urgency can be based on some factor that is in your control (such as: "I can only buy 3 houses this month"); or, urgency can be based on some factor that is up to your audience (such as: the sooner you want to get out from under this frustrating and costly property, the sooner you should contact me).

Urgency should be built all the way through your sales copy — in the **H**eadline, the **A**nxiety section, the **R**emedy section, the **P**roof section, and the **O**pportunity section.

Here are some tips to add Urgency into your copy:

Always include some component of urgency in your copy. This can be challenging but it will make your copy more effective.

Pick one type of urgency (which I listed above), or maybe two at the most, and highlight it all the way through your copy. Avoid the temptation to stack up multiple reasons because that can seem very forced. You can stack other things (like benefits) but urgency looks more authentic when there are only one or two strong reasons to act now.

Give a very clear time limit. If you are using a website or email, consider using one of those countdown timers, or links that expire.

What happens if you are contacted after your urgent time expires? For sellers, you may want to still do the deal, since you only get one shot at them. But for buyers, you may want to say, "Sorry, you're too late on this deal" to train your buyers that they need to act fast. (This is optional but I recommend it.)

Use this space to write additional notes or ideas that apply to you:

Copywriting Power Matrix—Engagement (E)

The fourth part of the sales copy component that makes up the Copywriting Power Matrix is the **E**ngagement.

	T	R	U	E
H				X
A				X
R				X
P				X
O				X

People are inundated with marketing. Constantly. And it's not just your competitors who are sending them similar-looking postcards or emails, your readers are inundated with marketing in every aspect of their life.

That means, you need to work extra hard to make sure that they read *your* marketing. Therefore, your copy needs to be engaging to hold their limited and distracted attention.

Engaging copy can be short or long, funny or serious, simple or complex, just text or video or some combination… but it just needs to get the reader to stick with the copy.

Engagement can be built all the way through your sales copy — in the **H**eadline, the **A**nxiety section, the **R**emedy section, the **P**roof section, and the **O**pportunity section.

Here are some tips to add Engagement into your copy:

Be interesting and entertaining. To paraphrase the insight from one well know copywriter: your writing should be the most interesting thing that your audience reads all day.

Every line of copy should be reviewed to make sure it moves the reader forward and is necessary. Cut it out if it's not.

Use surprise and the unexpected to capture their attention. Say something that shocks them (but be careful not to offend them; you should just be surprising), or say something in an unusual way.

As questions in your headlines and then answer those questions in your copy.

Number your paragraphs, even if it is not actually sequential, and that will encourage people to read all the way through (although this tends to work better if you have 15 or fewer paragraphs).

Include images that are compelling or unusual, and tie them into your key points through explanations in the copy.

Use this space to write additional notes or ideas that apply to you:

Summary

Whew! That was a long chapter but believe me, it will be worth it. Every time you want to write something, build this Copywriting Power Matrix and dig in. You'll find it a really valuable guide that takes all the guesswork out of copywriting. Ultimately, this Copywriting Power Matrix of 4 columns and 5 rows (20 cells in total) work together to create a tool that directs your thinking and research, which then becomes a single place for you to put all your research and notes, which then becomes a "map" of your sales copy. Once you've drawn the map, you can then sit down and start writing.

BONUS: The Copywriting Power Matrix is one of the most important tools you'll use when creating your copy. Make sure you get the chart and other additional resources at:
RealEstateInvestingCopywriter.com/bonus/playbookbonus

Look, many investors who are just starting out can't afford my services but still need the services of a copywriter. That's why I wrote this chapter: to educate some investors about why they need to hire me, *or* to help some investors know exactly what they need to find in a different copywriter, *or* to equip some investors (especially those who are just starting out or can't afford my services) to do the work on their own.

And once you have copy written (from another copywriter or on your own) you can always hire me to take a look at it and make sure it will work for your situation.

Learn more about my copywriting critique service here:
RealEstateInvestingCopywriter.com/copycritique

CHAPTER 14: ACTION PLAN: HOW TO BUILD AND DEPLOY EVERYTHING IN THIS BOOK TO GET IT WORKING FOR YOU

You've just read *a lot* of information. Chapter after chapter of strategies and tactics. Your head might be spinning. After all, what I'm sharing is the accumulated knowledge and skills acquired from years of being involved in investing, and years of marketing—all condensed into a few chapters. My goal here is to give you the tools to get a strong foundation and a fast start, and then point you in the direction of other great ideas and resources to take it to the next level.

But there's so much in the book, you might be wondering: how do I start? Where do I start? So, this chapter is meant to be an action plan to get you moving forward to deploy and growing.

Simply put, start at the beginning of the book and go through chapter by chapter. However, that might look slightly different for various investors, depending on how experienced you are:

If you are an investor who is new to investing: you have an advantage of just jumping in and going through the strategies in this book to get your first marketing deployed. In your case, just start at the beginning and work through chapter by chapter. Do what it says in the first chapter then go on to the next chapter. By the time you get here, you're ready to deploy!

If you are an investor who runs an existing business: you may be wondering: "should I scrap everything and start over?" Some investors may choose to do that but other investors don't have that privilege because they need to be producing deals right now while their marketing improves. So the decision comes down to the following

- For existing businesses, if you can put your deals on pause for a couple of weeks to focus on the information in this book, you may want to do that. Just pause all your marketing efforts and dig into this book for a week or two, level up your marketing and return to doing deals.

THE REAL ESTATE INVESTING COPYWRITER'S PLAYBOOK

- For existing businesses, if you can't put your deals on pause for a couple of weeks, then continue using your existing marketing but make changes as you go through each chapter, adjusting your existing marketing and funnel while it is running.

The Real Estate Investor's Action Plan: Putting It All Together

Here's the simple step-by-step action plan. Just follow these pieces and refer back to previous chapters to complete them.

From chapter 2
- ☐ Identify all your target audiences (for all your seller target audiences and your buyer target audiences).
- ☐ Create detailed write-ups of each one.

From chapter 3
- ☐ Identify the most important "WIIFM+ROI" acronyms for each of your audiences.

From chapter 4
- ☐ Identify your competition, including direct and indirect competition, as well as the competition of inaction.
- ☐ Figure out how you will sell against each of them.

From chapter 5
- ☐ Determine how you will specialize/differentiate to stand out from the competition and attract the right people in your target audience.

From chapter 6
- ☐ Build your story.
- ☐ Create your character.
- ☐ Nail down your voice.

From chapter 7
- ☐ Create your brand.
- ☐ If you have been investing for a while with an existing brand, identify the places in your business where your brand needs to change, and change it.

From chapter 8
- ☐ Identify your business model.

THE REAL ESTATE INVESTING COPYWRITER'S PLAYBOOK

From chapter 9
- ☐ Draw out your ideal sales funnel for each of your seller *and* buyer target audiences (if you are a new investor, you may need to guess at this, then tweak as you go; if you are an existing investor, you may consider building off of what's working for you now).

From chapter 10
- ☐ Get a blank notebook and schedule time to write in it regularly to build your list and deepen the relationship. (This will probably cause you to go back to your sales funnels to adjust those).

From chapter 11
- ☐ Identify your Must-Have marketing tactics and start pulling them together. Do this for each of your target audiences. You can complete a lot of these pieces based on what you've already covered in the book so far but if any of that marketing requires copywriting to finish it off then you'll finish them shortly when you get to chapters 12 and 13.
- ☐ For one-off things (like a website or bandit signs), just do them all them all right now.
- ☐ For ongoing things (like emails or blog posts), do 1-3 months of content, but avoid doing much more than that or else it will bog you down in content creation instead of doing deals.
- ☐ Don't worry about the May-Want marketing tactics just yet but schedule some time in (perhaps quarterly) to revisit the list of May-Wants and implement one.

From chapter 12
- ☐ Identify the key motivations of each of your target audiences and add that information to your target audience write-ups.

From chapter 13
- ☐ Use the Copywriting Power Matrix to complete any of the writing needed on your Must-Have marketing pieces that you started a couple of steps above

Following this checklist will help you go step-by-step through the information in this book to give you everything you need for your real estate investing business. And once you have it, then what do you do with it?

> **BONUS**: Get a downloadable version of this checklist here:
> RealEstateInvestingCopywriter.com/bonus/playbookbonus

The Real Estate Investor's Action Plan: Releasing It To The World

Now you're here ready to start putting everything out there into the world so sellers and buyers can contact you. However, here's where investors can get caught up if they aren't ready: *The best thing to do is to implement everything in reverse order of what your target audience will experience.*

So, looking at your sales funnel, build it from the bottom to the top. For example, let's say your sales funnel is a simple one like this:

1. You put up bandit signs and send out postcards.
2. People call your virtual assistant to book an appointment or they look at your website to book an appointment.
3. You show up at their house at the scheduled time to make an offer.
4. You sign the papers and close the deal.

The best approach is to implement it in reverse order:

1. Pull together the deal-closing paperwork and put it into a folder.
2. Pull together any educational or sales material you need for when making an offer, and put it into a folder.
3. Hire a virtual assistant and give him or her the sales script they need, and create your website.
4. Create bandit signs and postcards, and then post the signs and mail the postcards.

The advantage of this approach is: once you implement your marketing, everything else is all done and ready to go (compared to the other way of doing things: if you start marketing but don't even have a virtual assistant to answer the phone, well, there's nothing in place for when someone calls).

The disadvantage of this approach is: many investors can get caught up in content creation and wanting everything perfect and complete before they get started. I would caution you against that mindset. Just create good content that can be put to work for you and then modify on the fly. That way, even your imperfect marketing can be working to get you deals while you make it better.

CHAPTER 15: THE 4 STEP SEQUENCE TO IMPLEMENT EVERYTHING CONFIDENTLY AND GROW YOUR INVESTING BUSINESS

I've given you the strategies to get started and to grow. Now the next part is up to you. In this chapter I'll share the four step sequence to implementing everything successful so you can grow your investing business.

No matter where you are in your investing career, this will help you move forward: if you are not doing deals yet, or if you feel like you've been in "getting-ready-to-be-an-investor" mode for a while, or if you have done a few deal but want to grow your investing business, figure out where you are and do the next thing.

This is the same process I use in all of my businesses, and it's the simple sequence I run my clients through whenever I work with them—whether I'm just starting to work with them or I've been working with them for years, I always come back to this sequence.

Step #1. Take Action Today

The very first thing I'd tell every investor (and aspiring investor) is to take action today. There are so many people who want to invest, or who are stuck in a seemingly eternal cycle of learning (but never implementing), or who are investing more slowly than they want to be... and the remedy for that is to take action.

Stop looking for the perfect action or the next piece of information or the missing link before you start... *just get started*.

The times in my life when I achieved my goals (no matter what those goals were) were the times when I moved forward even though I didn't know all the steps. I knew the first couple of steps and went from there, figuring it out on the fly.

Simply work on what you know until you reach a hit a wall and can't move forward, then solve that step and keep moving forward.

That's how I invested in my very first cash-flowing property: I had some money to invest and I knew I wanted to buy a cash-flowing property from a wholesaler that I knew and trusted. So I called him up and he told he how he'd need to get paid (by wire transfer). That's when I hit my first wall and had to figure out how to access my money and get it to him (which took a couple of extra steps because my money was in Canada and the wholesaler and investor were in the US). But, step-by-step, I worked through it, and got moving forward again until I found out that I needed a special account for the property management company to deposit rental checks. A new wall! I worked on that until it was solved and the checks started coming in.

… and so on.

That's how I suggest you work as well. Do that in all aspects of your investing business, including the strategies that I share in this book.

If you ever find yourself stalling for whatever reason, it's usually because of one of the following reasons:

- You are scared about moving forward
- You don't know what your next step should be
- You are too busy to take action

No matter which of the above three reasons apply to you, here's what to do: simply break down that step into very, very steps until you have a step that is so small and fast and easy to do (and not scary).

One example might be: if you need to send out postcards to motivated sellers. It's a big step and a lot of investors get hung up on it. Problem is, it's not actually a step, it's a number of steps. You need to break it down into smaller steps:

1. Figure out what parameters you need to build a list of motivated sellers
2. Find a place to rent a list
3. Contact them and give them your list of parameters
4. Get a price quote from the company
5. Purchase the list
6. Receive the list as a spreadsheet.
7. Find a postcard that you can send to your list
8. Find a couple of companies who will print and mail your postcards
9. Get price quotes from each company
10. Compare quotes
11. Choose a company
12. Send them the spreadsheet (from step 6) and the postcard (from step 7)
13. Pay them
14. … and so on

When you divide a big, confusing, scary step into many smaller steps, it becomes far easier and faster to do and much more actionable. And even if the steps are simple but scary, and it's ultimately your fear holding you back, you can still follow this same process! For example, if you have a list of motivated sellers' phone numbers, and you need to call them but your fear is holding you back, just break it down into simple steps:

1. Pour a glass of water
2. Sit at my desk
3. Make a list of questions to ask the people who answer the phone
4. Get the list of phone numbers to call
5. Dial the first number on the list
6. If they answer, introduce myself (if they don't answer, dial the next number on the list, until someone answers)
7. Ask the first question
8. Listen to the response
9. Ask the second question
10. Listen to the response
11. … and so on

Suddenly it becomes much easier to do.

If you are moving forward and taking action, great! If you are ever delayed for any reason, then simply break out that step into smaller steps. Scary steps become much more manageable, complex steps become much simpler to do, and if you're too busy to do everything then you can at least find a few things that you can do now to move forward.

But the bottom line is: take action now. Take action, even if imperfect, and don't ever stop.

In this book, I've given you a ton of actions to take, so go through this book and do them all.

Step #2. Focus.

One challenge that is common among many investors I meet is the "shiny object syndrome." I believe that a lot more investors would make a lot more money if they could only focus on something for longer than two minutes.

Unfortunately, many investors become interested in something (such as a certain type of investing or a certain style of marketing) and try it out for a week or two, only to give it up and replace it with something else. So many investors give up too soon!

Rather than trying one thing and moving to another, pick a system, strategy, process, sales funnel... *and then commit to doing that for an entire year.* It might seem excessive when compared to the typical approach. And there will be many investors who read that and say, "but what if I commit to doing something and it doesn't work?" (ironically, these are often the same investors who do something and then do something else and don't give the first approach time to work). Well, you can commit to something for a period of time, and get it dialed in and then refine it (see step 3) and there's a good chance you can figure it out.

Unfortunately, many investors reading this (even those who agree with the wisdom of the above paragraphs) will still jump from one approach to another because they don't want to miss out on the opportunity... yet by not dialing in any approach, they are giving up on massive amounts of opportunity!

Choose one approach—just one!—and go through this book with that approach, and take action. If you find yourself going through this book one month as a wholesaler and then next month as a rehabber, and then the month after that as a note investor, and then the month after that as a mobile home park investors... well, that should be the warning sign that you need to focus.

Get that approach dialed in with consistency and good habits. Schedule your action steps into your calendar and create a spreadsheet that tracks results. Just get it dialed in to the point where you are comfortable with it.

Choose one approach and dial it in. Period. Mark your calendar and stick with it for a year. Yes, you can refine and improve that approach as you go but make sure you stay focused.

Step #3. Refine.

Once you have chosen one approach, get it dialed in and start trying to do a deal. As you go, modify and refine your approach.

Refining happens by testing and measuring results. Don't expect to hit a homerun right from the very first time you deploy your marketing. (I frequently turn down people who want to hire me if they are looking "for a script to a video that will go viral", or for a postcard that will give them 30% response rates on the very first mailing. Ummm... no. You only get to those results by testing and improving).

Testing is simple: Pick the thing you want to test (such as a postcard), and mail a batch of your baseline postcards. (In the industry we call this "the control"). Then also, make one change on your postcard (such as the color or the headline—just choose *one thing* to change) and mail an equivalent batch as the control.

Then, measure the response rates of each. Did more people call you back on your control postcard or on the new one? Did the increase in callers actually turn into an increase in deals?

The better postcard becomes the control (so, either your original control postcard remains the control, or your new postcard becomes the control) and you mail it again, along with a postcard with just one more new change.

This is called "A/B testing" or "split testing" and basically you are measuring your control against one small adjustment, and then looking at measurable results to determine which performed better.

I always recommend measuring a couple of metrics:

- Did your change create a greater response?
- Did the greater response turn into more deals?
- Did the increase in deals create more profit?
- Did you enjoy the results of this change?

Most copywriters will think that those four questions are too many to ask when measuring results but here's what I've seen: measuring *just* the response is short-sighted because what if you created a postcard that turned into a better response but those responses weren't actually better deals for you? (Maybe you changed a headline that simply increased the number of tire-kickers, or maybe you got more deals but they were a huge amount of work compared to the deals you got through your control).

I'm a big believer in creating an investing business that you love, not just one that makes money, so if you change up your marketing and suddenly start doing more deals but you hate doing those deals then you need to rethink your approach.

When split testing, make sure you only ever test one thing at a time. Otherwise, how will you know which change created the biggest impact? If you change the color of the postcard and the text of the postcard, how will you know if it was the color or the text to change?

Here are some of the things you'll want to split test in your investing business:

- Types of direct mail (postcards versus yellow letters versus some other types of direct mail)
- Different target markets
- Headlines, text, and color of direct mail
- Days of the week you send the direct mail
- Calls to action
- Website design
- Website headlines or text

- Different messages on your voicemail
- Brand design
- Social media (Facebook versus Twitter versus LinkedIn, etc.)
- Images (you versus images of your target audience)
- Days of the week to post

The list goes on and on but this is a good start and will keep you busy testing for a very long time.

One more thing I want to address: some investors don't test because they think it's expensive. However, I think this is a mistake. If you send out postcards and do one deal from it, and then test again and don't do any, well you can go back to the first way and keep doing one. But test again and you might find that you discover a way to start doing two deals from your mailings, or even three. The "cost" of testing is more than made up for by the greater results over the long-term.

Remember: everything is a test so even if you send out postcards and they don't deliver any responses, it wasn't a failure; you invested in a test and received knowledge that you can use for the future. You learned something, and now you can refine based on that knowledge.

Step #4. Scale

The fourth step is to scale your business. Once you get things dialed in and you start getting data to help you make improvements, then you'll need to scale. After all, your consistency (from the Focusing step) and your improvements (from the Refining step) should create more deals for you, so you'll need to grow your investing business to ensure that you can keep up.

In this step you'll want to scale in the following ways:

- Create systems that will help you become more efficient in what you do
- Automate some of the steps using software
- Delegate and outsource some of the steps to get it out of your hands

Eventually, you may get to the point where you are the visionary in your business but team members and software are doing the majority of the work for you. (Even if you still want to be active in your business, handing off some of the bigger pieces to someone else allows you to put more of your attention into the aspects of your investing business that you want to work on!)

Scaling used to scare me because I liked having control over my business but then I learned that I could have even more control over my business, *and spend more time doing the things that I loved to do*, by systematizing and outsourcing a lot of the work.

Look, if it's still early days for you, don't worry about this. But if you've been investing for a while, there's a good chance you want to make your work a bit easier, and scaling your business with team members and automation will help.

Summary

In my experience, every investor is at one of these four steps. You need to figure out where you are and look at what needs to happen next. Perhaps you're an aspiring investor who has not yet taken action… perhaps you're an investor who needs to focus… perhaps you're an investor who is focused and has a good approach all dialed in but now needs to refine it… perhaps you're an investor who has it dialed in and is refining but now needs to scale up.

This chapter is true for your branding and marketing; it's also true for many other aspects of your investing business too.

If you've read through this chapter and see yourself stuck at one stage and needing to move to the next, get in touch and let me know because I may have some contacts or recommendations who can help you. I meet a lot of investors, and I get access to a lot of investing resources, so I might be able to make a suggestion or an introduction of some software, resource, tool, or mentor who can get you moving forward.

BONUS: By the way, make sure you check out what I'm doing over on social media, including Facebook, Instagram, and YouTube. I share different stuff on each of those places. Find all my accounts here: RealEstateInvestingCopywriter.com/social

Good copy is an investment into your business.

PART 5: BEST PRACTICES

Parts 1 through 4 covered all the basic foundational pieces that you need to create and deploy great marketing. You're ready to go! But to help you even further, I've included two more chapters that will show you powerful, compelling tips and best practices that you can use when marketing to sellers and buyers.

These are useful tips and insights that are specific to sellers and specific to buyers. Use them to get your marketing dialed in at a higher level!

CHAPTER 16: BEST PRACTICES AND EFFECTIVE STRATEGIES FOR MARKETING TO SELLERS

In this chapter I'll share some of the tips and tricks I've developed and tested over the years in my own real estate investing business and in the investing businesses of my clients. I should add the disclaimer here that these work in specific situations and you should always think about what aspects may or may not apply to your business and adjust your approach accordingly. And always test, because things change and not everything transfers in exactly the same way to every market or to every seller audience.

This chapter will gather together many of the aspects of branding, marketing, and copywriting that you've read and will share them tactically here.

As I often say: real estate investing is one of the few industries where the entrepreneur has to "sell" a seller in order to build up their inventory before you can sell to a buyer. So these tips and tricks will help you do just that…

Watch Your Language

When building a brand and offering to buy a seller's house, make sure you use the word "house" instead of "home".

A "house" is a structure that can be bought or sold. A "home" is an emotion and a sense of belonging and family. People have a lot of emotions wrapped up in their home. So choose your words carefully—in your marketing and when speaking to sellers in person—and avoid using the word "home". You'll just make it that much more challenging to buy their house because they may be willing to part with the structure but they'll be reluctant to sell you their home.

It's okay to use the word "property" when talking to sellers and in some of your marketing but don't use it in your branding because most people aren't looking for that when they are looking for a solution.

Use the word "buy" instead of "purchase" or "invest". "Buy" is simple to understand. A word like "purchase" puts more emphasis on the transaction; a word like "invest" highlights that you intend to make money off of it.

"We buy houses" is the best phrase to use because it is simple to understand and say, and it keeps the focus on the solution that the seller is looking for. However, be aware that there may be potential trademark issues with that phrase. Consider using a variation on that phrase.

Another great idea is to add a benefit term, such as "fast" or "quick" or "we pay cash". Examples include: "Fast House Buyers" or "We Pay Cash For Houses" or "We Buy Houses Fast".

And, if you are focused on one market, consider using the name of that market in your branding, such as "We Buy Cleveland Houses Fast". However, be aware that there are two challenges to this approach—the first challenge is that you need to be sure to choose a term that your sellers are actually going to understand (if no one in your area knows the county name then don't use your county name in your brand); the second challenge is that it may limit you if you want to move into a different market

There Are Many Different Sellers

Many investors start with a single website that basically says "we buy houses". Problem is, the reasons that different motivated sellers may have for selling could be quite different—a burnt out landlord wants to sell for one reason, a person in financial difficult wants to sell for a different reason, a woman who is going through divorce and just wants to be rid of the painful memories of her house wants to sell for a different reason, and a person who has retired and wants to extract equity out of their house so they move into a retirement facility wants to sell for yet a different reason.

It's hard to market to each of these completely different audiences on the same site! Sure, they want the same outcome but they will respond to different benefits and you build rapport with them in different ways. For that reason, you may want to consider one of the following strategies when deciding how to structure your website. You may want to consider the following:

Start with a generic "we buy houses" site. This is a great start, and very fast and simple to get up and running. If this is all you get running at first, that's a good start. However, remember that it's hard to speak specifically to each target audience this way, so I actually recommend that you start with this but add the following:

Add different pages for each target audience so you can speak directly to their different motivations. When sharing on social media, be sure to share your landing page for the target audience you're speaking to. So, if you write a post to retiring owners, you might link to example.com/retiring and if you write a post to burnt out landlords, you might link to example.com/landlords. That way, you target each one with one page.

Multiple sites that each speak to a specific audience. As you grow, you can slowly shift to this approach, which is a longer-term approach that is more work and comes at a higher price. However, it has some advantages like: you can create really simple, memorable domain names, you get better search engine optimization potential, you get the ability to brand in a way that connects to each target audience, and you get the ability to slice off and sell pieces of your business to other investors.

Frankly, this is too much work for you to do in the early stages of your business. Do this approach once you have your business up and running and you are looking to refine your business and scale it.

I like both approaches and they can be effective. Each one has its advantages and disadvantages so, in my opinion, it comes down to your ability to invest in them. The first one will get you up and running faster, the other one will allow you to scale even bigger.

What Kind Of Direct Mail To Send?

The eternal debate among investors, and a question I am asked just about every day on the phone, is: "should I send postcards, yellow letters, or more traditional white-letter/white-envelope direct mail?"

In general, I like sending postcards the best because they are inexpensive and have a 100% open rate; you don't have to rely on the seller opening an envelope. However, in highly competitive markets, you might have a lot of other investors sending postcards. (This is especially true after one of those event gurus comes to town and holds a free event and tells everyone to mail postcards).

If that's the case, try sending your postcards on different colored paper (yellow, pink, or green) and switch up the words a bit so that your postcard isn't identical to every other postcard out there.

If your sellers are getting a lot of postcards, then switch to an enveloped letter—of which there are typically two kinds:

- An informal "yellow letter"-style letter. Send the yellow letter to sellers who are in foreclosure or pre-foreclosure, have tax delinquency, or have a burdensome house that is in need of repair. These people tend to respond well to the informal nature of a yellow letter.

- A formal letter (one that is on white paper and typed). Send these more formal letters to sellers who are absentee owners, older sellers, foreign sellers, burnt out landlords, inherited houses, and those facing divorce or who need to sell because they are moving quickly.

I have the following rule of thumb: *For sellers who are selling for financial reasons (i.e. they are in financial distress), be informal; for sellers who are selling for other reasons (i.e. they don't want to deal with the property anymore or they are too busy or emotionally distraught), then a more formal letter is better.*

To someone in financial distress, a formal (typed) letter in a formal (typed) envelope usually brings pain. They're used to receiving this kind of letter from banks or bill collectors so they feel a lot of negative feelings about them or have even developed the habit of throwing them out unopened. So, if you think your audience hates receiving formal letters, send them informal ones.

On the other hand, some audiences respond much better to formal letters, such as older sellers and foreign sellers, who attribute greater respect and credibility to a typed letter than the informality of a yellow letter.

These are just my general recommendations but you should test it out for yourself because every market and every target audience may be different. Think of these as educated guess starting points. Try these approaches and test.

Contact And Communication

When you are connecting with sellers, avoid email. Use phone or text as much as possible. There may be times when you need to use email (such as: when you send them a contract) but in general email is not a great way to communicate with sellers: open rates are low and your emails can end up in the spam folder or in an "Offers" tab (such as in Gmail). I will use email to follow-up with a seller but almost never as a first contact.

Plus, sellers who are in greater motivational need to sell will call or text because they want to end their pain right now. Sellers who email tend to be tire-kickers looking to see your offer to decide if they want to think about selling.

(That's not to say you shouldn't collect seller emails; just be aware that it's not the best way to connect with them.)

Competition

As you work with sellers, be aware of what competition you're facing. In nearly every situation you are facing at least the following competition:

- Selling through an agent. This is the traditional approach and it's a default approach for many people.
- Selling on their own.
- Selling to another investor.
- Doing nothing.

Remember that you are selling against all of these options so make sure you are addressing each one in your marketing and your education. And ultimately, that's what you need to do: educate sellers on what their options are and what the best one is for them. If you don't firmly believe that your option is the best option then stop investing and do something else. On the other hand, if you do firmly believe it, make a gigantic list of all the reasons that someone would want to do business with you and weave those reasons into all of your marketing.

Video: Do More Video

As a copywriter, most people think that my work revolves around the written word. And, for the most part, it does. I write postcards and letters, websites, and emails. But in my work I encounter all different types of marketing. One of the biggest opportunities for investors who are trying to find sellers is video.

Simply put: you probably aren't doing enough videos right now. Do more of them.

YouTube is the second largest search engine on the planet, right after Google. And you probably know this already: Google owns YouTube and they embed YouTube search results into Google search results. As if that isn't compelling enough, today's internet users are consuming more videos than ever before—massive amount of video each and every day on platforms including YouTube, Facebook, Instagram, and elsewhere.

However, real estate investors are simply not doing enough videos. So it's become one of my standard sentences that I say in just about every interaction with every seller: "How many videos are you doing?" (and after they tell me,) "You should probably do more."

Not only are your sellers consuming videos, Google's ranking of YouTube videos allows you to rocket to the top of the Google searches very quickly, even in highly competitive markets.

So, how many videos should you be doing? Here's what I suggest: Do 2-3 videos each and every day. Shoot videos that are just a couple of minutes each (so, in total, you might spend less than 10 minutes shooting videos! It's so easy!) and then upload them to YouTube with relevant keywords like "We Buy Houses In [and the name of your city] For Cash." In fact, you should start a whole channel all centered on that very keyword and make your YouTube channel the definitive source of videos on this keyword.

Do this every day.

Yes. Every. Single. Day.

The first week will be fine.

The second week will seem boring and repetitive to you.

Most will have stopped by then.

But this is a long-term play. Think weeks and months, not days. Just keep generating content. You'll rank, you'll get viewers, you'll get calls from sellers, you'll turn those calls into deals.

So, what should you do on your videos? I'd mix it up but consider some of the following:

- Videos of you doing walkthroughs of houses
- Videos of you talking to sellers
- Videos of you answering FAQs that sellers have
- Videos of you sharing insights that are relevant to your sellers
- Videos of you talking about the pain points that sellers have

… And every single video needs to end with a call to action for them to call you.

Even though I'm a copywriter and I believe strongly in the power of copy to grow an investing business, I think videos are the overlooked, very-low-hanging fruit for nearly every investor.

Summary

These are just a few tips to guide you as you think about marketing to sellers. If you want more tips and ideas, be sure to check out my blog at RealEstateInvestingCopywriter.com.

CHAPTER 17: BEST PRACTICES AND EFFECTIVE STRATEGIES FOR MARKETING TO BUYERS

As with sellers, I've developed a few tools and tricks over the years to help real estate investors market and connect with buyers.

Two Kinds Of Buyers

Investors typically work with two kinds of buyers, so keep this in mind while marketing to them:

- **Retail buyers (or tenants)**. These are people who buy real estate from you that they will live in. It includes people who buy the house up-front (with a mortgage), as well as rent-to-own tenants, and even rehabbers who want to live in a house while they fix it up.
- **Investor-buyers**. These are people who want to acquire a property so they can generate a financial return from it by renting it or flipping it. This could include a cash investor who has the funds up-front, or someone who has money in a 401k to acquire property, or it could include investors who need to use a mortgage or loan to invest.

In general, investors will be marketing to the following groups (again, these are rules of thumb and there may be variations or slight differences; but this is a starting point).

- **If you're a wholesaler**: you'll probably be marketing to investor-buyers who want to acquire a property that they will flip or hold for cash flow.
- **If you're a turnkey wholesaler**: you'll probably be marketing first to tenants to put one into your property and then to investor-buyers who will acquire the cash-flowing property.
- **If you're a rehabber/flipper**: you'll probably be marketing to retail buyers who will pay top dollar for your beautifully renovated house.

- **If you're a cash flow investor**: you'll probably be marketing to tenants (or rent-to-own tenants) who will live in your property for a while and pay you while they do.

Retail buyers and investor-buyers each respond to their own types of marketing…

For retail buyers: you'll find that retail buyers typically are looking for safety, comfort, and convenience (i.e. proximity to work, schools, or whatever is important to them) within their price range.

If your buyers have a family, or who want to start one, then they're more motivated to buy and they're less likely to move (compared to a single guy who can pack everything he owns into a backpack). Therefore, if you focus on your home's family-friendly and family-safe features, you'll tend to attract better buyers. In your marketing, highlight features such as:

- The family demographics in the area (i.e. if there are a lot of families with babies there)
- Parks and playgrounds nearby
- Proximity to schools
- Proximity to grocery stores
- Number of daycares in the area (especially the number of daycares that have spaces available!)

Another component to consider is envy. People love it when other people are envious of them—whether family, friends, or neighbors. If you are a rehabber/flipper who renovates houses to sell to retail buyers, consider building in features that will allow you to highlight envy in your marketing. I have a client who buys some of the worst properties in a neighborhood and then builds them into the nicest properties in the neighborhood. His homes really are something that a buyer's friends or family would be extremely envious of. His marketing shows that angle off, and it's no surprise that his houses sell for top dollar.

Tenants and rent-to-own tenants will be similar to most of the list above, except for the envy piece. (And that makes financial sense for you, too, since you probably don't want to create a rental property that has a lot of high-end features anyway). For your tenant and rent-to-own tenants, highlight safety, comfort, convenience, and those family-friendly features. (For rent-to-own tenants, you may consider also highlighting the additional factor of being able to get into a safe, comfortable home without the necessity of having great credit.)

Of course features are only part of the offer. You'll want to highlight the benefits. For example: it's a feature to say, "there's a playground just across the street," but your marketing should state that but move it further into the benefit of that marketing with something like, "there's a fun playground with a climbing structure just across the quiet street which means you'll love looking out your kitchen window and seeing your children playing and laughing for hours with their neighborhood friends."

For investor-buyers: it's a different approach. They won't be living there so you don't need to highlight the safety, comfort, or convenience of the property. These are investors so you need to point out how the property is perfect to generate a return (which depends on the reason they're buying).

For example, if you're a wholesaler who is wholesaling the property to a rehabber then you'll want to highlight how the property is structurally sound, so they can make fast cosmetic changes only and see a big gain. Or, if you're wholesaling or selling a property to a cash flow investor then you'll want to highlight how much consistent cash flow they get each and every month.

It's all about the return on investment (ROI) as the primary feature. There are secondary features that you might want to highlight as well, including: low expenses, an up-and-coming area, a fully managed property, and a long-term tenant.

Of course, these are *features*. To turn them into *benefits* you need to talk about what it means for your investor-buyer. A cash flow return isn't just consistent income, it's passive income that allows them to quit their job and fund an early retirement so they can do anything they want. A gain from the sale of a rehabbed property could be a six-figure payday that means they don't have to work for the rest of the year.

Want More Buyers? Do These Four Things

In the previous chapter I talked about how videos were a low-hanging fruit for investors looking to find more sellers. I've made a similar observation for investors looking to find more buyers. There are three things you should do that most investors aren't doing... and it might seem weird for me to say this as a copywriter but it's what I've experienced so I'm passing it along:

1. Start a podcast. Podcasting is big and it's going to get bigger. If you're serious about building an audience, start a podcast.

2. Record more videos. Just like podcasting, video is big and going to get bigger. Start shooting more videos.
3. Write a book. It doesn't have to be a big book but 100+ pages will help to set you apart as an investor worth listening to.
4. Go to conferences. Conferences can have a potentially high cost so it prohibits some people from going but nothing has accelerated my businesses like the connections I've made at conferences. From investing to copywriting, and all my other businesses: they've each grown massively when I attended conferences. (They don't have to be investing conferences; just go where your best buyers will likely hang out. For example, maybe go to a stocks and securities conference and chat with stock market investors; or go to a chiropractic conference and set up a booth to meet chiropractors looking to invest their money and cut back on the amount of time in their practice.)

Now, if you've been paying attention and reading this book diligently then you'll probably realize that I have not just described four random things to do for buyers but rather four very strategic things that work together as a platform. In other words: you can start your podcast and radio show, build up an audience, leverage it further with a book, and then bring that expertise with you to conferences. These are powerful and work together.

Your Brand: Be Authentic But Not Boring

One last tip about finding buyers: be authentic but not boring.

- **Be authentic**: there are way too many investors who are faking it until they make it by pretending to be ultra-successful even when they are not. Don't be the guy who goes to the exotic car dealership and takes a photo beside a luxury sports car and pretends the car belongs to them. Instead, be yourself. If you're new, that's okay. Leverage the experience you do have to grow. There's always something you can leverage. Even if you are brand new you can leverage that by saying, "Learn with me as I grow." There are a million entrepreneurs who have started that way.
- **Don't be boring**: Some people work so hard to avoid being flashy and inauthentic that they swing too far to the other side of the spectrum: they end up being boring. They mistake boring for authenticity. It's not. You can be authentic and also fun,

crazy, silly, smart, or whatever you are. Figure out who you want to work with, find the connection between that audience and your own personality, and leverage it.

Your brand to attract buyers should be compelling and fascinating and authentically you.

Summary

These are just a few simple tips to guide you as you work with buyers. If you want more tips and ideas, be sure to check out my blog at RealEstateInvestingCopywriter.com.

I have a special book-writing service for investors, but it's a secret because I don't do it for everyone who asks!

Ideas If you need help figuring out what your book should be about or how it can help you grow your business, I can give you some ideas and recommendations.

Writing: If you have an idea for a book (even a vague idea) I have a team of book writers who will actually ghostwrite your book for you. This is a way to rapidly bring your book to life, even if you don't have time to write it yourself. It's your words and your ideas and your name as the author, but my team will craft it for you into a book you can be proud of.

Publishing: Once you have a book, you need to get it published! Whether you wrote the book yourself or got my team to do it, I can help you with publishing. I have published numerous books for myself and for clients and have some systems and resources in place to help.

The best place to start is to email me and put "book" in the subject line, then tell me what you need:
aaron@realestateinvestingcopywriter.com

NOW IT'S TIME TO TAKE ACTION…

As an investor, your job is clear: find sellers, acquire properties, find buyers, sell those properties; be sure to add value all the way through.

That's it!

But getting that job done is more challenging because sellers and buyers have many options and the marketplace is crowded. There are many options to connect, which means that sellers and buyers are facing a lot of "noise" to find the right solution (meanwhile, you're trying to be everywhere at once to connect).

Worse yet, your money is wasted as you try to yell into the noise, and your time is wasted when you end up talking to the wrong people. I hear these complaints from investors every single day. It's frustrating. You don't want to be marketing 24/7… you want to be doing deals, making money, and living the lifestyle that you dream of living.

So, **make this book your action plan**. Go through it chapter by chapter to build an investing business that connects confidently and successfully with the right sellers and the right buyers.

Keep this book on your desk, within easy reach, to refer to over and over. Use it as a starting point and make sure you are connected with me on my site, through my VIP email list, and on Facebook and Instagram and YouTube—where I share my best up-to-date field-tested strategies for finding more sellers and buyers. Make it a habit to spend just 15 minutes a day reviewing marketing strategies that I share in one of these channels, and apply that lesson in your business. 15 minutes a day doesn't seem like much but day after day after day adds up and will have a profound cumulative effect.

There are so many opportunities out there in many markets (even small markets and even in highly competitive markets). I see it every day. These strategies will help you find those opportunities and profit from them.

It's time for you to get started. It's time to take action. It's time to build your investing business and serve sellers and buyers. You got this! I can't wait to watch you grow to the next level.

BONUS

Don't forget! I share a whole bunch of resources, strategies, recommendations, and downloadables here:

RealEstateInvestingCopywriter.com/bonus/playbookbonus

ABOUT AARON HOOS

Aaron Hoos is a real estate investor and the world's only exclusive real estate investing copywriter. He works *only* with real estate investors to help them find more sellers, more buyers, more students, more readers, more listeners, more of anything.

Aaron grew up around investors and investing—his father was a contractor and his parents rehabbed the houses they lived in. For a while, Aaron thought his life was headed in a different direction (thanks to an undergraduate degree in the humanities), an after college job at a real estate developer's office brought him right back into the industry.

Armed with an undergraduate in the humanities, a stock broker's license, and an MBA in strategy, Aaron brings an unlikely but valuable combination of academic knowledge to his work.

But of course it's not all theory: Aaron owns cash-flowing real estate in both the US and Canada, he has rehabbed residential real estate, and been involved in many other types of investing including mobile home parks, commercial deals, syndications, and more.

Aaron also owns or co-owns other businesses because he can't sit still for very long.

So, why does he still "write for hire" as a copywriter for investors? Because that's his calling, his life's work, the topic that occupies the most space in his mind, *and* because he meets investors every day who need help connecting the world of investing with the world of marketing.

Aaron's client's run the gamut from total newbie to highly respected investors with large operations, including Kent Clothier, "The Real Estate Guys" (of Real Estate Guys Radio), InvestorCarrot (and many of their clients), Jason Hartman, Mark Evans DM,DN, Joe Evangelisti, and many others.

Aaron lives in Canada with his wife Janelle. When he's not writing, he loves to travel, read, and drink coffee.

CONNECT WITH THE
REAL ESTATE INVESTING COPYWRITER

Website: RealEstateInvestingCopywriter.com
Blog: RealEstateInvestingCopywriter.com/blog
VIP List: RealEstateInvestingCopywriter.com/join
Social: RealEstateInvestingCopywriter.com/social
Contact: RealEstateInvestingCopywriter.com/contact

Facebook: Facebook.com/realestateinvestingcopywriter
Instagram: Instagram.com/REIcopywriter

REAL ESTATE INVESTING COPYWRITER

THE DEFINITIVE RESOURCE FOR INVESTORS WHO WANT TO MASTER THEIR MARKETING

Do you want more seller and buyer leads that turn into more deals? Do you want to get laser-focused on proven, field-tested strategies rather than wishing, wondering, or costly trial and error? Do you want someone to help you create content who actually knows the market and knows exactly what your sellers and buyers are thinking?

If so, there is only one source for the latest research, insight, resources, and step-by-step strategies to help you create more effective marketing.

- Read the latest blog posts
- Improve your marketing ROI
- Find resources or services
- Connect on social
- See what's working now
- Join the VIP list

RealEstateInvestingCopywriter.com

1.

2.

MAKE SURE YOU'VE JOINED MY VIP LIST

My VIP list is the exclusive place to get access to me, my latest strategies, and to get first notice of my availability.

Read the latest research and strategies for real estate investors—I share it with my VIP list before I share it anywhere else. And, my VIP list is the first place that gets access to my availability for copywriting. You'll also get great deals, insider information, marketing resources, and introductions to my friends and network.

Plus, you can tell me where you're doing deals and I often try to make introductions if I think there's a fit!

RealEstateInvestingCopywriter.com/join

THE REAL ESTATE INVESTING COPYWRITER'S PLAYBOOK

LEVEL UP YOUR EXISTING MARKETING WITH A COPY CRITIQUE

Not everyone can afford my copywriting services. I understand that. As well, many investors already have marketing content working for them already and they're not looking for *new* content.

That's why I also offer copy critiques: I will analyze your existing copy (including sales letters, VSLs, postcards or direct mail, landing pages, email sequences, etc.) and give you specific insights to help increase its effectiveness.

I'll run it through my proven critique processes and share my observations, and recommendations: you'll get my notes and a recording so you or your team can make changes.

RealEstateInvestingCopywriter.com/copycritique

FIND PODCASTS, PROMOTE YOUR PODCAST, AND FIND GREAT PODCAST GUESTS

Podcasts and video shows are big... and growing. If you think they're big now, just wait: Gary Vaynerchuk says they'll be even bigger.

Today's internet user consumes audio and video at an unprecedented rate, and real estate investors are stepping up to deliver great podcasts and video shows to hungry audiences!

If you are an investor who wants to find the next great podcast...
If you are a podcasting investor who wants to promote your podcast or find guests...

The Real Estate Investing Podcast Directory is the web's only definitive source for investing-focused podcasts.

RealEstateInvestingPodcastDirectory.com

REAL ESTATE INVESTING COPYWRITER

~ COMING SOON ~

THE REAL ESTATE INVESTOR MARKETING SHOW

Want to get great marketing insight on video? This is one of the most common requests I get from investors. Well, after a long wait, I'm finally doing it!

(*Actually what happened was: I built a video recording studio in my home… and then decided to sell my home and move, and my new home doesn't have a studio yet.*)

Frankly I'm at the point where I will just start recording videos anyway because I'm sure you'd rather have great insight even if it's not a slick production.

RealEstateInvestorMarketingShow.com

Made in the USA
Middletown, DE
12 May 2019